St. Augustine on
Marriage and Sexuality

Selections from the Fathers of the Church

VOLUME 1

St. Augustine on Marriage and Sexuality

EDITED BY

ELIZABETH A. CLARK

The Catholic University of America Press
Washington, D. C.

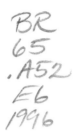

Copyright © 1996
The Catholic University of America Press
All rights reserved
Printed in the United States of America

The paper used in this publication meets the minimum
requirements of American National Standards for Information
Science—Permanence of Paper for Printed Library materials,
ANSI Z39.48-1984.
∞

LIBRARY OF CONGRESS CATALOGING-IN-PUBLICATION DATA
Augustine, Saint, Bishop of Hippo.
    St. Augustine on marriage and sexuality / edited by Elizabeth A.
Clark.
        p.   cm. — (Selections from the Fathers of the church ; v. 1)
    Includes bibliographical references and index.
    1. Marriage—Religious aspects—Christianity.   2. Sex—Religious
aspects—Christianity.   I. Clark, Elizabeth A. (Elizabeth Ann),
1938–   .   II. Title.   III. Series: Fathers of the church. Selections ;
v. 1.
BR65.A52E6   1996
241'.63—dc20
96-8089
ISBN 0-8132-0866-1 (alk. paper)
ISBN 0-8132-0867-x (alk. paper)

JESUIT - KRAUSS - McCORMICK - LIBRARY
1100 EAST 55th STREET
CHICAGO, ILLINOIS 60615

For Annabel Wharton
Scholar, teacher, friend

CONTENTS

ABBREVIATIONS

St. Augustine on
Marriage and Sexuality

INTRODUCTION

When in 1930 Pope Pius XI issued his encyclical *Casti Con-nubii* ("On Chaste Marriage," although the title is often rendered in English as "On Christian Marriage"), he used as the structuring device for his letter the three "goods" of marriage elaborated by the Church Father Augustine over fifteen hundred years earlier. According to the Pope, the good of offspring precluded a Christian's use of contraception, sterilization, or abortion; the good of fidelity stood against any pre- or extra-marital sexual relations; and the good of the "sacramental bond" disallowed divorce to Catholic couples except in rare circumstances.[1] The very fact that a head of the Catholic Church in the twentieth century could rest his case so firmly on the teachings of an author who lived a millennium and a half earlier indicates the signal importance of Augustine's writings on marriage and sexuality for the centuries to come.

To be sure, Christian writers had addressed issues pertaining to marriage and sexuality before Augustine's era.[2] Although the Gospels themselves do not provide a systematic discussion of these topics, they do represent Jesus as teaching on the subject of divorce and on "becoming a eunuch for the Kingdom of Heaven" (Matthew 19.12)—topics that were much discussed in later Christian literature. Paul, in 1 Corinthians

1. An English translation of *Casti Connubii* can be found in *Seven Great Encyclicals,* ed. William J. Gibbons, S.J. (New York/Paramus: Paulist Press, 1963), pp. 77–117.
2. A good overview, with selections, is provided by David G. Hunter, *Marriage in the Early Church* (Minneapolis: Fortress Press, 1992).

1

.7, had claimed that celibacy is a better option for Christians "because of the impending distress" (usually now interpreted to mean the expectation of the imminent coming of the Kingdom of God), but advised married couples to remain as they were, practicing abstinence from sexual relations only for periods of prayer. He believed that, when one partner in a marriage converted to Christianity while the other did not, it was preferable for them to remain together, but he did not forbid divorce if such an arrangement proved unworkable. Paul, in 1 Corinthians 7, also counseled Christian widows to remain unmarried: they would be happier in their single state, he proposed. Yet Paul's preference for celibacy over marriage was contested by the author of the Pastoral Epistles (1 and 2 Timothy and Titus), who wrote as if he expected most Christians to be married. Advising younger widows to remarry and produce offspring (1 Timothy 5.14), the author of these letters did not recommend the preservation of virginity, as had Paul.

The second and third centuries saw Christian writers offering both incidental comments and full-scale treatises on such topics. Various second-century commentators condemn in passing "unnatural" sex acts and abortion, but praise Christians who were living to old age in chastity.[3] Moreover, in response to the alleged Gnostic denigration of marriage and reproduction, Clement of Alexandria at the turn of the third century produced a substantial treatise extolling marriage. In it he both claimed Paul for the ranks of the married and took pains to explain why Jesus had not married, if marriage was in manifest accord with God's wishes for the human race.[4] On the other hand, some of the Apocryphal Acts produced within the same era represent celibacy as the superior Christian life: thus they depict their heroines as defying family, fiancés, and husbands in their attempts to commit themselves to Christian chastity. Thecla, the heroine of the *Acts of Paul and Thecla*, for example, refuses to marry her fiancé after she hears Paul preaching the message of Christian asceticism; Drusiana, heroine of the *Acts of John*, is buried in a sepulchre for two weeks by her husband

3. See, for example, Justin Martyr, *Apology* I.27; Athenagoras, *Plea on Behalf of Christians* 34.
4. Clement of Alexandria, *Stromateis* III, esp. 6.49, 53.

when she refuses to accede to his sexual requests.[5] Here, Christian commitment is explicitly identified with sexual renunciation.

In the next centuries, the impulse to asceticism became even stronger in Christianity.[6] By the later third century, Christians were fleeing to the desert (or simply staying at home) to practice ascetic renunciation. The reasons for the bourgeoning of the ascetic movement in this period are not entirely clear: was asceticism an escape from an overly hierarchalized (and "sacramentalized") Church? from a Church to which thousands of "laxer" converts had flocked in the recent past? from a larger society whose mores might be thought to corrupt the Christian's spirit and whose tax burden was viewed as oppressive? Whatever the reasons for the ascetics' retreat, by the early fourth century, organized communal monasticism had been instituted, and by the later fourth century, some Christian writers were outrightly disparaging the married life in comparison with celibacy. Yet the strongly ascetic strand in the Christianity of this era could not be carried too far: Christians recalled that in Genesis 1 God had commanded Adam and Eve to "reproduce and multiply" and had pronounced his blessing on their relationship. Moreover, Christians feared that they might be identified with such heretical groups as the Manicheans, who condemned reproduction out of their belief that physical bodies were the product of an evil deity who used the "trick" of procreation to further entrap in materiality the particles of Light defeated in an original cosmic battle. Over against such views, Christians resolutely championed the notion that God had created human bodies as good. It was in this setting of Christian debates over asceticism and the rejection of Manichean views that Augustine began to develop a sexual ethic that, despite the nuances and reinterpretations he gave it in

5. English translations of these and other Apocryphal Acts can be found in Edgar Hennecke and Wilhelm Schneemelcher, *New Testament Apocrypha,* tr. R. McL. Wilson (Philadelphia: The Westminster Press, 1965), II: 353–364, 244–254.

6. For a convenient overview of these developments, see Peter Brown, *The Body and Society: Men Women, and Sexual Renunciation in Early Christianity* (New York: Columbia University Press, 1988).

the course of his lifetime, became decisive for all later teaching in the Christian West on issues of marriage and sexuality.

Augustine was born in 354 in North Africa to Patricius, a minor local official of the Roman government, and Monica, a devout if somewhat superstitious Christian who labored hard to bring her husband and son into the Christian fold.[7] Recognizing his son's intelligence, Patricius planned a career for Augustine that might have brought him considerable public recognition in Roman society. To this end, Augustine received the standard literary and rhetorical training given at his time to young men of appropriate social and economic status; in due course, he became a teacher of rhetoric and eventually was invited to serve as the public orator of the city of Milan. Yet the further development of his promising career was cut short when, after a long interior struggle, Augustine felt called to a Christian commitment and abandoned his secular position.

The chief points that had dissuaded Augustine from adopting Christianity more readily, he reports in the *Confessions*, were two: that the Scriptures seemed poorly written compared with the Latin literature he loved and taught; and that his strong sexual desires could not find free enough expression within the strict Christian sexual ethic.[8] The first of his problems was overcome when he learned to interpret Scripture allegorically, largely through the model of Ambrose, bishop of Milan, whose allegorical exegesis of the Bible, coupled with a Platonizing worldview, raised Christian teaching to an intellectual level that Augustine found challenging.

The second issue—that of his allegedly irrepressible sexual desires—remained more problematic, according to Augustine's testimony in the *Confessions*.[9] He had taken a concubine while in his middle teens and with her produced a son, Adeodatus, within the first year of their union. Despite their rela-

7. The most readable biography of Augustine remains Peter Brown, *Augustine of Hippo: A Biography* (Berkeley/Los Angeles: University of California Press, 1969). We know far more about Augustine than we do about most other Church Fathers, since in his *Confessions* he details his remembrances of the first three decades of his life.

8. Interestingly enough, Augustine seems never to have entertained the notion that he could be a devoted Christian *and* be married at the same time.

9. See selections below, pp. 13–17.

Introduction

tionship of nearly fifteen years, they never had another child—
a fact that some interpreters credit to the contraceptive techniques that Augustine hints he had learned from the Manicheans during his years as a Manichean Auditor.[10] Although
Augustine appears to exaggerate the uncontrollability of his
sexual impulses—he himself reports that he remained faithful
to his concubine throughout all their years together[11]—he
nonetheless saw the tussle between the "flesh" and the "spirit"
as a marked characteristic of human life. That conflict strongly
influenced his understanding of sin and salvation once he converted to Christianity.

After Augustine abandoned the Manichean camp and became a Christian, he proposed to write on the contrast between
Manichean sexual ethics and those of Catholic Christians: this
he accomplished primarily in two treatises of the late 380s, *On
the Morals of the Manicheans* and *On the Morals of the Catholic
Church*. In these works, he contrasted the ascetic views of some
Manicheans, supposedly motivated by a hatred of the tainted
body, with those of ascetic Catholics who restrained themselves
from love of God. He also noted the Manicheans' allowance of
sexual relations for the lower rank of their adherents, the Auditors, if—and only if—these adherents adopted various contraceptive measures. The anti-reproductive stance of the Manicheans was one that Augustine came to combat strongly to the
end of his days: indeed, for Augustine, the major purpose of
sexual relations in marriage was the procreation of children.[12]
If Adam and Eve had not sinned in the garden of Eden, he
came to believe, the desire to engage in sexual acts motivated
only by lust would never have occurred: procreation would
have remained the only purpose of sexual intercourse. As he
developed his sexual ethic in the years thereafter, Augustine
emphasized that any form of sexual activity which automati-

10. For a detailed discussion of Augustine's views on contraception, see
John T. Noonan, Jr., *Contraception: A History of Its Treatment by the Catholic Theologians and Moralists*. Enlarged edition (Cambridge/London: Harvard University Press, 1986), ch. 4.

11. See below, p. 17.

12. For selections from Augustine's writings pertaining to the topics that
follow, see below, chs. 3 and 4.

cally ruled out the possibility of conception, such as anal or oral sex or same-sex relations, was to be condemned as "against nature." Likewise, he came to think that the sexual desire experienced even by married couples was sinful to some lesser degree—a sinfulness that would be excused by God if the couple did not engage in any contraceptive practices or "unnatural" sexual acts, and remained good Catholic Christians in other respects.

Yet the sexual and reproductive dimensions of marriage were not the only ones that Augustine addressed. In his treatise of 401, *The Good of Marriage,* he also proposed that there is a "sacramental bond" forged between Christian couples at the time of marriage that linked them indissolubly together: thus, he argued, Christians could not divorce, even if one of the parties committed adultery.[13] (In such a case, he later explicated, the innocent party might separate from the adulterous spouse, but divorce was not to be permitted.[14]) In this respect, Augustine's teaching was more rigorous than Roman law of the period, which permitted the initiation of divorce by either the wife or the husband.[15]

In addition, at various points in his writings, Augustine briefly addressed the topic of the faithful companionship that husband and wife might offer to each other.[16] Thus he can speak of Eve as "Adam's only companion" and speculate on the devoted partnership they might have shared if they had not sinned. Likewise, insofar as Augustine held that the essence of marriage lay in the "consent" that the spouses gave to each other, not in the sexual act itself (as some other Christian think-

13. See below, pp. 49–50, 55–56.

14. See Augustine's arguments in *On Adulterous Marriage* 1.3.3.; 1.7.7; 1.12.13; 2.10.10.

15. For marriage law under fourth-century Christian emperors, see Judith Evans Grubbs, *Law and Family in Late Antiquity: Constantine's Legislation on Marriage* (Oxford: Oxford University Press, 1995). A shorter overview appears as "'Pagan' and 'Christian' Marriage: The State of the Question," *Journal of Early Christian Studies* 2 (1994) 361–412.

16. For a discussion of this issue and the ones that follow, with references to Augustine's texts, see Elizabeth A. Clark, "'Adam's Only Companion': Augustine and the Early Christian Debate on Marriage," *Recherches Augustiniennes* 21 (1986) 139–162. See below, pp. 43, 51, 72–73.

ers believed), he pointed the way to an understanding of marriage that rested less on physical relationship and more on the acts of mind and will that brought the couple together. Augustine used the example of Joseph and Mary to demonstrate that "consent" was the essence of marriage: Mary and Joseph were truly a married couple, he argued, even though they never had sexual relations. Augustine did not, however, elaborate much on these non-sexual aspects of his understanding of marriage; especially in his later battles with Pelagian opponents, the sexual dimensions of the married relationship took center stage in the discussion.

If in his early years as a Christian, when he was combatting the Manichean "determinism," Augustine had championed the freedom of the will to choose and perform the good, as he matured he became progressively less eager to advance this point. It was probably through his study of Paul's Epistle to the Romans in the middle and later 390s that he began to adopt a more skeptical view of the will's ability to extricate itself from sinful thoughts and behavior: humans (even baptized Christians) throughout their lives struggle against the "desires of the flesh." There was a mystery to human sinfulness that was not explainable on rational grounds. Sin was not just the effect of inadequate teaching or bad habits that could swiftly be remedied with instruction and virtuous practice; some dark spot remained in the human heart and will, even after the cleansing provided by Christian Baptism.[17]

Augustine came increasingly to see this "darkness"—represented in lust and in humans' embarrassment at the seeming uncontrollability of their sexual organs—as a result of the initial sin in the Garden of Eden. That the first couple rushed to cover their naked bodies after the sin suggested to Augustine that something untoward had occurred in regard to their sexual organs and desires that had not been present before.[18] From our later perspective, we might posit that Augustine perhaps pointed to these events as symbols of the problematics of human relationship; nonetheless, his interpretation of Genesis

17. For a discussion of the early stages of Augustine's "darkening vision," see Brown, *Augustine*, ch. 15.
18. See below, pp. 76, 92, 101.

1–3 was taken by later opponents as having practical consequences for the thought and behavior of Christians concerning
marriage and sexuality. Indeed, his views were adopted by
many later Christian teachers to enforce a conservative sexual
ethic.

Augustine's encounter with Christian debates over asceticism in the 390s merged with his continuing meditation on
Paul's picture of human sin in Romans and on Genesis 1–3 to
lead him away from an unnuanced championing of human
freedom and of marriage. In particular, he tried to stake a middle ground between the claims of resolutely ascetic writers who
hinted that marriage and reproduction were unworthy expe-
riences for Christians, and those, in contrast, who made out
that no preference was to be given to ascetic living. Over
against the staunch ascetics, Augustine praised marriage for
the "goods" it produced—although increasingly he would remind his readers that the sinful force of lust remained even in
those couples who struggled mightily to lead lives of Christian
virtue. But over against those who assigned no superiority to
celibate living, Augustine agreed with many Christian writers
of his day that Paul had been correct in awarding first place to
celibacy, even while he acknowledged, quoting the words attributed to Jesus in Matthew 19.11, that "not all could receive"
such a teaching.[19]

In the last two decades of Augustine's life, he was pushed
by Pelagian opponents to state his position on marital and reproductive issues most clearly and fully. In many ways, Pelagius' views resonate with Augustine's early anti-Manichean
teaching: Christians should be encouraged to strengthen their
wills so that they can choose and perform the good, since no
evil impulse or power prevents them from doing so. Thus
Christians are free to choose lives of sexual purity and restraint.[20] For the followers of Pelagius, who further developed
his views on marriage and sexuality, there is no inherited guilt
that corrupts the human heart and will. Espousing a "devel-

19. See selections from *The Good of Marriage* and *Holy Virginity*, pp. 42–69.
20. For some selections from Pelagius' *Letter to Demetrias* that illustrate
these points, see *Theological Anthropology*, ed./trans. J. Patout Burns (Philadelphia: Fortress Press, 1981), pp. 39–55.

opmental ⸻ggested
that child ⸻pying bad examples,
which har ⸻ habits. But this state of affairs was
correctable, even in adulthood: to claim that darkness remained in the human spirit even after Baptism suggested to some Pelagians that Augustine had inadequately estimated the power of the Christian Sacraments, especially Baptism, and was veering dangerously close to a "Manichean" view of the wickedness of human nature.

Against the Pelagians, Augustine developed a doctrine of Original Sin that was to remain long influential on Christian theology, even when later modified to provide stronger encouragement for moral effort.[21] Augustine's mature views on Original Sin went, in brief, as follows: although the first couple had been created with free will and had the ability to keep from sinning, once that first wrong choice was made by Adam, following Eve, humans lost their ability to choose the good. This disability applied not just to Adam and Eve: all their descendants were implicated in the sin.[22] Thus each child who comes into the world is inevitably tainted with the guilt of this sin and deserves future damnation unless the guilt is erased by the grace of God. Even Christian parents bring forth unregenerated children, the "cultivated olive" engendering the "wild olive," as Augustine expressed it, borrowing Paul's analogy in Romans 11.17–24. Two of the decisive results of the Original Sin, according to Augustine, were to render humans mortal and dominated by lust throughout their lives. Although Baptism can mitigate the effects of Original Sin, the human body remains resistant to rational control, and death still awaits us at the end—although Augustine believed that an everlasting heavenly reward awaited those Christians to whom God had granted his predestining grace. Here was a developed inter-

21. Selections from Augustine's anti-Pelagian writings that address these topics can be found below, pp. 72–78, 87–88, 96.

22. Augustine's theory of the transfer of Original Sin probably *should* have led him to the view that souls were transmitted along with bodies in the process of conception—but he never espoused this view, remaining undecided until the end of his life how best to explain the soul's origin and its unio body.

pretation of Paul's words in Romans 5–7 concerning the sin of
Adam and the disobedience of our bodily members.

The followers of Pelagius reacted strongly to this aspect of
Augustine's teaching. To them, Augustine's explanation of sin
seemed to condemn marriage and reproduction.[23] Had God
been mistaken in arranging the world to include two sexes, by
implanting sexual desire in them and blessing the reproductive
act? Of course not! To Pelagian opponents, Augustine's views
were not just deluded, they were dangerous, strongly reminis-
cent of the Manichean condemnation of the body and reproduction. In his last battle with the Pelagian Julian of Eclanum
—detailed in Chapter Four below—Augustine struggled to uphold the position that marriage and reproduction *were* goods,
despite the views he simultaneously expressed concerning Original Sin's transmission and the wickedness of lust. Some schol-
ars now think that Augustine, under attack by such Pelagians,
may have softened his position on these issues in his later years,
conceding the possibility that (hypothetically) there could have
been an innocent *libido,* sexual desire, in a sinless Garden of
Eden.[24]

The selections from Augustine's writings in this volume are
apportioned into four chapters. In the first are contained passages that pertain to Augustine's own life and illustrate some
of his positive and negative models of marital relationship.
Chapter Two sets forth Augustine's responses to the Manichean teachings on the body, reproduction, and marriage,
mostly from his early years as a Christian. The third chapter
contains materials marking Augustine's reaction to the ascetic
debates within late fourth-century Latin Christianity. The last
chapter illustrates Augustine's mature sexual and marital ethic
that he elaborated in the midst of—and in reaction to—arguments with Pelagian writers. The chapters thus document
the chronological development of Augustine's views on mar-

23. For a discussion of Augustine's argument with the Pelagian Julian of
Eclanum on these points, see Elizabeth A. Clark, "Vitiated Seeds and Holy
Vessels: Augustine's Manichean Past," in *Gnosticism and Images of the Feminine,*
ed. Karen King (Philadelphia: Fortress Press, 1988), pp. 367–401.

24. See, for example, Peter Brown's discussion of the new Letter 6* of
Augustine in *The Body and Society,* pp. 423–425.

riage and sexuality. For the dating of particular treatises, I have largely followed the chronological tables provided in Peter Brown's *Augustine of Hippo*.

The footnotes internal to the selections were compiled by the original translators.

There follows a list of books and articles in English that the reader may consult for discussions of the above topics.

Suggestions for Further Reading

Bavel, T. J. van. "Augustine's View on Women." *Augustiniana* 39 (1989) 5–53.

Bonner, Gerald. "Some Remarks on Letters 4* and 6*." In *Les Lettres de Saint Augustin decouvertes par Johannes Divjak*. Paris: Études Augustiniennes, 1983, pp. 155–164.

Børresen, Kari Elisabeth. *Subordination and Equivalence: The Nature and Role of Woman in Augustine and Thomas Aquinas*. Tr. Charles H. Talbot. Washington, D.C.: University Press of America, 1981.

Brown, Peter. *Augustine of Hippo: A Biography*. Berkeley/Los Angeles: University of California Press, 1967.

———. *The Body and Society: Men, Women, and Sexual Renunciation in Early Christianity*. New York: Columbia University Press, 1988.

———. "Sexuality and Society in the Fifth Century A.D.: Augustine and Julian of Eclanum." In *Tria Cordia: scritti in onore di Arnaldo Momigliano*. Ed. E. Gabba. Como: New Press, 1983, pp. 49–70.

Brown, Peter, et al. *Augustine and Sexuality*. Berkeley: The Center for Hermeneutical Studies in Hellenistic and Modern Culture, 1983.

Clark, Elizabeth A. "'Adam's Only Companion': Augustine and the Early Christian Debate on Marriage." *Recherches Augustiniennes* 21 (1986) 139–162.

———. "Heresy, Asceticism, Adam and Eve: Interpretations of Genesis 1–3 in the Later Latin Fathers." In *Genesis 1–3 in the History of Exegesis: Intrigue in the Garden*. Ed. Gregory A. Robbins. Toronto: Edwin Mellen Press, 1988, pp. 99–133; also in Elizabeth A. Clark, *Ascetic Piety and Women's Faith: Essays in Late Ancient Christianity*. Studies in Women and Religion 20. Lewiston/Queenston: Edwin Mellen Press, 1986, pp. 353–385.

———. "Theory and Practice in Late Ancient Asceticism: Jerome, Chrysostom, and Augustine." *Journal of Feminist Studies in Religion* 5 (1989) 25–46.

———. "Vitiated Seeds and Holy Vessels: Augustine's Manichean Past." In Clark, *Ascetic Piety* [see above for full reference], pp. 291–

349, and in *Images of the Feminine in Gnosticism*. Ed. Karen L. King. Philadelphia: Fortress Press, 1988, pp. 367–401.

Coyle, John Kevin. *Augustine's "De Moribus Ecclesiae Catholicae": A Study of the Work, Its Composition and Its Sources*. Paradosis 25. Fribourg: University Press, 1978.

Driver, S. D. "The Development of Jerome's Views on the Ascetic Life." *RTAM* 62 (1995) 44–70.

Fredriksen, Paula. "Beyond the Soul Body Dichotomy: Augustine on Paul Against the Manichees and the Pelagians." *Recherches Augustiniennes* 23 (1988) 87–114.

Hunter, David G. "Resistance to the Virginal Ideal in Late Fourth-Century Rome." *Theological Studies* 48 (1987) 45–64.

————, ed., tr. *Marriage in the Early Church*. Sources of Early Christian Thought. Minneapolis: Fortress Press, 1992.

Lieu, Samuel N. C. *Manicheanism in the Later Roman Empire and Medieval China*. 2nd ed. Tübingen: J.C.B. Mohr (Paul Siebeck), 1992.

Markus, Robert A. "Augustine's Confessions and the Controversy with Julian of Eclanum: Manicheaism Revisited." In *Collectanea Augustiniana: Mélanges T. J. van Bavel*. Ed. B. Bruning et al. Leuven: Leuven University Press, 1990, pp. 913–925.

Miles, Margaret R. *Desire and Delight: A New Reading of Augustine's Confessions*. New York: Crossroad, 1992.

Noonan, John T., Jr. *Contraception: A History of Its Treatment by the Catholic Theologians and Canonists*. Enlarged edition. Cambridge/London: Harvard University Press, 1986, pp. 107–139.

Pagels, Elaine. *Adam, Eve, and the Serpent*. New York: Random House, 1988.

Wolff, Hans Julius. "Doctrinal Trends in Postclassical Roman Marriage Law." *Zeitschrift der Savigny-Stiftung für Rechtsgeschichte*. Romanistiche Abteilung 67 (1950) 261–319.

AUGUSTINE'S LIFE AND MODELS

Augustine's Confessions, *sometimes described as the first spiritual and intellectual autobiography of the Western world, provides the reader with valuable information about the childhood, youth, and young adulthood of this important Church Father. The work is, in effect, an extended prayer to God, who is the "You" of the text. To be sure, Augustine wrote the* Confessions *years after the events he describes (namely, between 397 and 401), so the account is a retrospective reconstruction of his earlier life. In this work, Augustine recalls his stormy youth and his eventual safe entry into the Christian Church. Many commentators think that Augustine's personal struggles with sexual desire colored his later views on such topics as the link between Original Sin and lust.*

Augustine represents his own adolescence as one marked by turbulent desire, which his father celebrated and his mother feared. How much better, he reflects in the Confessions, *it would have been for him to marry young and let his sexual desire result in the procreation of children:[1]*

BOOK TWO, CHAPTER 2

(2) What was it that delighted me, except to love and to be loved? But, the moderate relation of mind to mind was not maintained according to the bright bond of friendship; rather,

---

1. FOTC 21.34–37, emended by the editor.

the mists of slimy lust of the flesh and of the bubbling froth of puberty rose like hot breath beclouding and darkening my heart. It thus was not possible to distinguish the serenity of love from the dark mist of lust. Both [love and lust] seethed together in hot confusion, and swept foolish youth over the precipice of passions and engulfed it in a whirlpool of shameful actions.

Your anger prevailed over me, and I knew it not. I had grown deaf with the clanging of the chains of my mortality, a punishment for my pride of soul. I moved farther from You and You permitted it. Through my sexual sins, I was scattered and poured out, and my ebullience was dissipated; and You kept silent. O how late came my joy! You were silent then, and I still wandered far from You, through more and more sterile seeds of sorrow, proud in my debasement, disturbed in my weariness.

(3) Who might have tempered my wretchedness and turned to good use the fleeting beauty of each latest attraction, setting a limit to their delights, so that the flood tide of my youth might be broken upon the shore of the marriage bond? It might have been calmed and made content by the goal of procreating children, just as Your law, Lord, prescribes. O Lord, You who also fashion the offspring of our mortality and by a light touch of Your hand can blunt the thorns which have no place in Your paradise.[2] For Your omnipotence is never far from us, even when we are far removed from You. Or I might have listened more carefully to Your voice[3] thundering from the clouds: "Yet such will have tribulation of the flesh. But I spare you that,"[4] and "It is good for man not to touch woman,"[5] and "He who is unmarried is concerned about the things of God, how he may

2. See Gn 3.18 for the introduction of the "thorns" of labor and toil into the family life of Adam and his descendants. Augustine's later comment (DGnL 3.18.28; DCD 22.17) shows that he associates this verse of Genesis with Mt 22.30, where it is said that there will be no marriage in the future paradise of heaven. While the present passage stresses the difficulties of marriage, Augustine often wrote of the triple blessings of matrimony (mutual trust, offspring, and the sacramental union); see especially DGnL 9.7.12; CJ 3.7.14; and the whole treatise DBC.

3. This is the "voice" of Holy Scripture; cf. DGnM 2.3.5; EnP 56.11.17.

4. 1 Cor 7.28.   5. 1 Cor 7.1.

please God; but he who is married is concerned about the things of the world, how he may please his wife."[6] I might have more carefully listened to these words and, thus made a eunuch for the kingdom of heaven's sake,[7] I might have more happily awaited Your embraces.

(4) But miserable person that I was, I boiled over and left You, following the violence of my flooding passions.[8] I broke the bonds of Your lawful restrictions yet did not escape Your punishments. What mortal can? You were ever present, mercifully angry and befouling all my illicit pleasures with most bitter aversions, so that thus I might seek to enjoy inoffensive pleasure. Where could I have found this? Certainly not in anything outside of You, O Lord, not outside of You, "who makes suffering into a lesson,"[9] who strike that You may heal,[10] and who kill us lest we die apart from You.

Where was I, and how long was I in exile from the delights of Your household, in that sixteenth year of the life of my flesh, when, giving myself wholly to its service, I was controlled by the madness of sensuality, legitimate by human standards, but illicit in terms of Your laws? Nor were my parents concerned to cut short my downfall with matrimony; rather, they were wholly concerned with my learning to make as good a speech as possible and to be persuasive in the use of words.[11]

BOOK TWO, CHAPTER 3

(5) My studies were interrupted during that year, when I was brought back from Madaura,[12] a nearby city in which I had, as a boarding student, already begun the study of literature and public speaking; now the funds to pay the expenses of a longer

6. 1 Cor 7.32–33.
7. Cf. Mt 19.12.
8. Cf. S 199.3; "Do not follow the flood of the flesh. This flesh is indeed a river, for it does not stand still."
9. Ps 93(94).20. Cf. EnP *loc. cit.* for the justification of the English.
10. Cf. Dt 32.39.
11. The key to a good position in government service, during the late Roman Empire, was a training in rhetoric and law.
12. The present Mdaourouch, a town in Numidia, some twenty miles south of Augustine's birthplace. Madaura was the home of the Latin writer Apuleius (2nd cent. A.D.), and remained a center of pagan learning.

stay in Carthage were being assembled, more by means of the ambition than the wealth of my father, who was a far from rich citizen of Tagaste.[13]

To whom am I telling these things? Not to You, O my God; rather, I tell them before You to my own kind, to the human race, no matter how few men may chance upon these pages. For what reason? So that I, and whoever reads this, may realize out of what depths one must cry unto You.[14] What is closer to Your ears than a heart that is penitent and a life founded on faith?[15]

Who did not then sing the praises of this man, my father, who in a manner beyond his ordinary means provided his son with whatever was needed for a long stay away from home for the sake of an education? Many far wealthier citizens never undertook such a task for their children. But, at the same time, this same father was quite unconcerned as to how I was growing up before You, or as to how chaste I might be, as long as I would be eloquent, a "dissertator," or rather, a deserter from Your tillage,[16] O God, who are the one, true, and good Lord of Your field, which is my heart.

(6) However, in that sixteenth year, when idleness was forced upon me by the limitation of my family's fortunes, I was free from school and lived with my parents. The thorn-bushes of lust grew above my head, and there was no hand to root them out. On the contrary, when my father saw me at the baths, growing into a young man and taking on the appearance of restless adolescence, he joyfully apprised my mother of it, as if this already gave him reason to rejoice in the hope of grand-children. His was the drunken joy in which this world becomes forgetful of You, its Creator, and loves Your creature in place of You,[17] as a result of the invisible wine of a will perverted and inclined to base things. But, You had already begun Your tem-ple and started Your holy dwelling in my mother's breast, while

13. The present Souk-Ahras, about fifty miles south of Hippo, which is the present town of Bône.
14. Cf. Ps 129(130).1: the famous lines, *De profundis clamavi ad te.*
15. Cf. Hb 2.4; Heb 10.38; Rom 1.17; and Gal 3.11.
16. Cf. 1 Cor 3.9.
17. Cf. Rom 1.25.

he was but a catechumen,[18] and that but recently. She thus experienced a rising feeling of holy fear and trembling for me; though I was not yet one of the faithful, she nevertheless feared the crooked ways in which they walk who turn their back and not their face to You.[19]

Augustine reports that, not long after, when he became a teacher of rhetoric, he took a concubine. With this woman, he produced a child in the first year of their long relationship.[20]

BOOK FOUR, CHAPTER 2

(2) . . . In those years, I lived with a woman,[21] not in a union which is called lawful, but one which restless and imprudent passion had sought out. Yet, there was but one woman and I was not unfaithful to her. But, I found in my own case what a difference there is between the moderated pleasure of conjugal union, which was mutually entered into for the generation of offspring, and a union of wanton love, in which a child is born but not wanted, though when born it compels one to love it.

As Augustine progressed in his career, his mother increasingly desired that he leave his concubine and contract a marriage with a young woman of good social background and suitable wealth; she thought that he would "settle down" and accept Christian Baptism after his marriage. The girl selected to be Augustine's bride was ten and a half years old; he was about thirty. In the Confessions, *he recalls this event:*[22]

BOOK SIX, CHAPTER 13

(23) I was unceasingly urged to take a wife. I had already proposed marriage and was now engaged, chiefly through the efforts of my mother, for, once married, the saving waters of Baptism might cleanse me. She was gladdened that I grew

18. Augustine's father, Patricius, remained a pagan until shortly before his death in 370.

19. Jer 2.27.

20. FOTC 21.75, emended by the editor.

21. This woman, whose name is never revealed, stayed with Augustine until shortly before his conversion in Milan.

22. FOTC 21.155–156, emended by the editor.

daily more adjusted to this goal and she noticed that her prayers and Your promises were being fulfilled in regard to my faith.

Of course, when at my request and because of her own desire, she prayerfully begged You daily, with the vehement cries of her heart, to show her something in a vision about my future marriage, You never would. She did see some vain and fanciful things, under the compulsion of the human spirit dwelling upon the matter, and she told me about it, but without the confidence she usually had when You showed something to her; rather, with contempt for this vision. For, she said that she could distinguish by means of some sort of savor, which she could not explain in words, the difference between Your revelation and the dreaming of her own soul.

The matter was kept going, however. A girl was spoken for who was almost two years younger than the age suitable for marriage; since she was pleasing, we waited.[23]

Augustine and his male friends planned to live together in a kind of intellectual commune, but the present reality and future prospect of wives dashed their scheme. Meanwhile, Augustine's concubine of many years was dismissed. By Roman law, fathers (not mothers) had custody over their children, so Augustine's son stayed with him. Yet Augustine reports in the Confessions *that he could not wait chastely until his young fiancée reached marriageable age, so he took another sexual companion.[24]*

BOOK SIX, CHAPTER 15

(25) In the meantime, my sins were multiplied. When the woman[25] with whom I had lived for so long was torn from my side because she was a hindrance to my marriage, my heart, to

23. Girls were permitted to marry at the age of twelve (Justinian, *Institutiones* 1.10.22); this girl must have been rather young. She and Augustine were never married, of course.

24. FOTC 21.157–158, emended by the editor.

25. The mother of Adeodatus appears to have been of such a social level that Augustine did not consider marrying her. It is evident that Monica did not care for her. Augustine has been criticized for his treatment of the woman, but we do not know the circumstances well enough to make a judgment.

which she clung, was cut and wounded, and the wound drew blood. She returned to Africa, vowing unto You that she would never know another man and leaving with me the natural son[26] whose mother she was.

But I, unfortunate, unable even to emulate a woman and impatient at the delay attendant upon waiting two years for the girl to whom I had proposed, because I was not a lover of marriage but a slave of lust, procured another woman—but not as a wife. Thus, it was as if the whole, or an increased, illness of my soul were sustained and continued, under the escort of a persisting custom, into the very realm of matrimony. Nor was that wound of mine healed, which had been made by cutting off the first woman; rather, after the fever and most severe pain, it began to fester, and, though the pain seemed cooler, it was more desperate.

Soon thereafter, Augustine states in the Confessions, *he experienced a dramatic call to conversion that resulted in his abandonment of marriage plans and his commitment to celibacy. In his recounting of this dramatic moment, Lady Continence triumphed over his desire to enjoy his former "toys," the sexual partners who still beckoned to him in his memory.[27] Many commentators have suggested that these years of inner turmoil over his sexual desires and conduct left a lasting impression on Augustine.*

In the following passage from The Good of Marriage, *composed in about 401, Augustine may be recalling his past experience with his concubine:[28]*

CHAPTER 5

(5) The question is also usually asked whether this case ought to be called a marriage: when a man and woman, neither of whom is married to anyone else, because of incontinence have intercourse with each other not for the purpose of procreating children but only for the sake of sex itself, with this pledge between them, that neither of them will have sex with anyone else. Yet perhaps not without reason this can be called

26. Adeodatus.   27. C 8.11–12.
28. FOTC 27.15–16, emended by the editor.

wedlock, if this has been agreed upon between them that this arrangement should last even until the death of one of them and if, although they do not have intercourse for the purpose of having children, they at least do not avoid it, so that they do not refuse to have children nor act in any evil way so that they will not be born. But, if both or either one of these conditions is lacking, I do not see how we can call this a marriage.

For, if a man lives with a woman for a time, but only until he finds another worthy either of his high station in life or his wealth, whom he can marry as his equal, in his very soul he is an adulterer, and not with the one whom he desires to find but with her with whom he now lives though not in a real marriage. The same is true for the woman, who, knowing the situation and willing it, still has sexual relations unchastely with him, with whom she has no vow as a wife. On the other hand, if she remains faithful to him and, after he has taken a wife, refuses to marry and is prepared to refrain absolutely from such an act, surely I would not lightly dare to call her an adulteress. Yet who would not say that she had sinned, when he knows that she had relations with a man though she was not his wife?

If from the union, however, she wants nothing except children and whatever she endures beyond the reason of procreation she endures unwillingly, surely this woman ranks above many matrons, who, although they are not adulteresses, nevertheless force their husbands, who often desire to be continent, to have sexual intercourse, not with any hope of progeny, but through an intemperate use of their right under the passion of lust, still, in the marriage of these women there is this good, that they are married. They are married for this purpose, that lust may be brought under a lawful bond and may not waver disgracefully and loosely. Lust has in itself a weakness of the flesh that cannot be curbed, but in marriage there is an association of fidelity that cannot be dissolved. Of itself, lust leads to immoderate intercourse, but in marriage it becomes a means of reproducing chastely. For, although it is disgraceful to make use of a husband for purposes of lust, it is nevertheless honorable to refuse to have intercourse except with a husband and not to give birth except from a husband.

Augustine held traditional views of correct female behavior. One feminine model he held up to his readers was that of his mother, Monica. In the Confessions, *he praises her for the meekly subordinate position she had assumed in relation to his father, Patricius:*[29]

BOOK NINE, CHAPTER 9

(19) Brought up in this modest and sober manner, made subject to her parents by You rather than to You by her parents, given in marriage when she reached a suitable age, she served this man "as her lord."[30] She was eager to win him for You,[31] speaking to him of You through her behavior, in which You made her beautiful, reverently lovable, and wonderful to her husband. Thus, she even put up with wrongs of infidelity, never permitting any dissension with her husband as a result of such a matter. She looked forward to Your mercy upon him, that he might become chaste as a believer in You.

Moreover, though he was outstanding for his kindness, he was also quick to anger. But, she had learned not to oppose an angry husband, either by action or even by word. Eventually, when she would observe that his mood had changed and become tranquil, she would seize the opportunity to explain her action to him, if, by chance, he had been irrationally disturbed. In short, while many matrons whose husbands were of milder disposition bore the marks of beatings, even in the form of facial disfigurement, and during friendly conversations they criticized the behavior of their husbands, she criticized their talkativeness, seriously reminding them, but as if it were a joke, that from the time that they had heard the reading of those contracts which are called matrimonial, they should have considered them as legal forms by which they had become slaves; accordingly, being mindful of their condition, they ought not to be haughty in relation to their lords. When they expressed amazement, knowing as they did what a bad-tempered husband she put up with, that there had never been any rumor or indication to suggest that Patricius[32] had beaten his wife, or

29. FOTC 21.247–250, emended by the editor.
30. Cf. Eph 5.21.
31. Her husband, Patricius, was a pagan for many years.
32. In [one] work (R. Pottier, *S. Augustin le Berbère* [Paris 1945]), the thesis

that they had quarrelsomely disagreed with each other, even for one day, they asked in a friendly manner for an explanation and she told them her way of getting along, which I have noted above. Those who adopted it were grateful as a result of their own experience; those who did not observe it continued to be annoyed at their subjugation.

(20) At first, too, her mother-in-law was stirred up against her by the whisperings of badly disposed servant-girls. But, she persevered in showing marks of respect, and this won her over by patience and gentleness, with the result that her mother-in-law spontaneously revealed to her son the meddling tongues of the servants, by whom the domestic tranquility between herself and her daughter-in-law was disturbed, and she expressed her desire that they be punished. So, after this, acting in obedience to his mother, in consideration of good order in the family and with concern for the harmony of them all, he had the culprits punished by whipping, in accordance with the recommendation of their denouncer. She promised that like reward should be anticipated by anyone who said anything bad to her about her daughter-in-law, in order to incur her favor. After that, no one made another attempt, and they lived together in a remarkably pleasant state of good will.

(21) You have also given to this good bondswoman of Yours, in whose womb You did create me, O my God, my Mercy,[33] the great capacity of serving, whenever possible, as a peacemaker between whatever souls were in disagreement and discord. Thus, when she heard from both parties a good many very bitter remarks about each other—the sort of things which bloated and undigested discord usually vomits up when the indigestion of hatred belches forth into sour gossip with a present friend about an absent enemy—she would not reveal anything about one to the other, unless it would be useful in reconciling them.

---

is maintained that Augustine's family is completely indigenous to North Africa. This is quite possible; in fact, there is no real evidence for the contention of many biographers that Patricius was of Roman descent. Many Africans took Roman names. However, Pottier's arguments are more the product of ethnic enthusisasm than scholarship. Cf. A. Dyroff 's note on Augustine's parentage, in L. Schopp, *Aurelius Augustinus Selbstgespräche* (Munich 1938) 114–118.

33. Ps 58(59).18.

This would seem but a small good, except that I have had sad experience with countless crowds of people who, through some dreadful and very widespread pestilence of sin, not only run to angry enemies with the statements of their angry enemies, but even add things which were not said. On the contrary, it should be little enough of an obligation for the man who is worthy of his species to refrain from starting or increasing animosities among men by evil talk, if, in fact, one does not even strive to extinguish them by good talk.

Such a person was she, under the influence of Your teaching as an inner Teacher in the school of her breast.[34]

(22) Eventually, she won her own husband over to You, right at the end of his earthly life, and she found no cause for complaint in him when he was now one of the faithful, such as she had borne when he was not yet in the faith. She was also a servant of Your servants.[35] Among them, whoever knew her found much reason in her for praising, honoring, and loving You, for one felt Your presence in her heart through the fruitful evidence of her saintly manner of life.[36] She had been the wife of but one man,[37] had made some return to her parents, had managed her own household in piety, and possessed a reputation for good works. She had brought up her children, being in labor with them[38] each time that she saw them wandering away from You. Finally, O Lord, she took such care of all of us, whom in Your bounty permit me to call Your servants—for, before she went to her rest in You we were already living in a group after receiving the grace of Your Baptism—that it was almost as if she were a mother to us all, and she served us in such a way that it was as if she were the daughter of us all.

34. This theme of Christ as the Interior Master is developed thoroughly in the dialogue *De magistro*.

35. Cf. Gn 9.25.

36. Monica is recognized as a saint in Catholic tradition; it is clear that she was so regarded by her son. Other examples of Augustine's esteem, which go beyond mere filial piety, are to be found in DOr 2.1 and DBV 1.10.

37. For the special position of widows in the early Church, cf. 1 Tm 5.3–16, phrases from which are here quoted.

38. Cf. Gal 4.19.

This view of matronly submission Augustine continued to hold in later life. At some undetermined point, he wrote to a married woman named Ecdicia, chastising her for her attempts to adopt a life of sexual and other forms of renunciation while she and her husband were still living together. Although the husband had apparently first agreed to live without sexual relations, he found that he was unable to keep his end of the agreement. Augustine was quick to praise a mutual and voluntary sexual abstinence in marriage—Mary and Joseph served as his models—but he strongly criticized such arrangements when one party (usually the husband) was unwilling or unable to adopt such a life. In Epistle 262 to Ecdicia, an otherwise unknown woman, he writes as follows:[39]

After reading your Reverence's letter and questioning the bearer on the points that remained to be asked, I felt a very deep regret that you had chosen to act so to your husband that the edifice of continence which he had begun to rear should have collapsed into the melancholy downfall of adultery by his failure to persevere. If, after making a vow of chastity to God and carrying it out in act and in disposition, he had returned to carnal intercourse with his wife, he would have been a source of grief, but how much more is he to be grieved over now that he has plunged headlong into a deeper destruction by breaking every bond and committing adultery in his rage at you, ruinous to himself, as if his perdition were a more savage blow at you! This great evil arose from your not treating him in his state of mind with the moderation you should have shown, because, although you were refraining by mutual consent from carnal intercourse, as his wife you should have been subject to your husband in other things according to the marriage bond, especially as you are both members of the Body of Christ.[40] And, indeed, if you a believer, had had an unbelieving husband,[41] you ought to have conducted yourself with a submissive demeanor that you might win him for the Lord, as the Apostles advise.

I say nothing of the fact that I know you undertook this state of continence, contrary to sound doctrine, before he gave con-

39. FOTC 32.261–269, passim.   40. Eph 5.30 and 1 Cor 6.15.
41. 1 Cor 7.13.

sent. He should not have been defrauded of the debt you owed him of your body before his will joined yours in seeking that good which surpasses conjugal chastity. But perhaps you had not read or heard or considered the words of the Apostle: "It is good for a man not to touch a woman, but for fear of fornication let every man have his own wife and every woman have her own husband. Let the husband render the debt to his wife and the wife also in like manner to the husband. The wife does not have power over her own body, but the husband; and in like manner the husband also does not have power over his own body but the wife. Defraud not one another except by consent, for a time, that you may give yourselves to prayer and return together again lest Satan tempt you for your incontinence."[42] According to these words of the Apostle, if he had wished to practice continence and you had not, he would have been obliged to render you the debt, and God would have given him credit for continence if he had not refused you marital intercourse, out of consideration for your weakness, not his own, in order to prevent you from falling into the damnable sin of adultery. How much more fitting would it have been for you, to whom subjection was more appropriate, to yield to his will in rendering him the debt in this way, since God would have taken account of your intention to observe continence which you gave up to save your husband from destruction!

But, as I said, I pass over this, since, after you had refused to agree to render him the conjugal debt, he agreed to this same bond of continence and lived in perfect continence with you for a long time. By his consent he absolved you from your sin of refusing him the debt of your body. Therefore, in your case, the question at issue is not whether you should return to intercourse with your husband, for what you both vowed to God with equal consent you ought both to have persevered to the end in fulfilling. If he has fallen away from this resolution, do you at least persevere in it with constancy. I should not give you this advice if he had not given his consent to this course. For, if you had never obtained his consent, no lapse of years would have excused you, but, if you had consulted me however

---

42. 1 Cor 7.1–5.

long afterwards, I should have made you no other answer than what the Apostle said: "The wife does not have power over her own body, but the husband." By this power he had already given you permission to practice continence and, for himself, undertook to practice it with you.

But there is a point which, I am sorry to say, you did not observe, because you should have given way to him all the more humbly and submissively in your domestic relationship since he had so devotedly yielded to you in so important a matter, even to the extent of imitating you. For he did not cease to be your husband because you were both refraining from carnal intercourse; on the contrary, you continued to be husband and wife in a holier manner because you were carrying out a holier resolution, with mutual accord. Therefore, you had no right to dispose of your clothing or of gold or silver or any money, or of any of your earthly property without his consent, lest you scandalize a man who joined you in vowing higher things to God, and had continently abstained from what he could demand of your body in virtue of his lawful power.

Finally, it came about that, when scorned, he broke the bond of continence which he had taken upon himself when he was loved, and in his anger at you he did not spare himself. For, as the bearer of your letter described it to me, when he found out that you had given away everything or almost everything you possessed to two unknown wandering monks,[43] as if you were distributing alms to the poor, he cursed them and you with them, and alleging that they were not servants of God but men, who creep into other people's houses, leading you captive[44] and plundering you, he indignantly threw off the holy obligation he had assumed with you. For he was weak and, therefore, as you seemed the stronger in your common purpose, he should have been supported by your love, not exasperated by your boldness. For, even if he was perhaps slower in being moved to almsgiving on a more liberal scale, he could have learned that also from you, and if he had not been affronted by your un-

43. That is, not attached to any monastery. They seem to have been plentiful in Africa, and were reprobated by Augustine in DOM 28.36. The Rule of St. Benedict called them *gyrovagues* and warned sternly against them.

44. 2 Tm 3.6.

expected extravagance but had been won over by the dutiful-
ness he expected from you, you could have done together even
this which you rashly did of yourself, and much more prudently, in more orderly and honorable fashion, with union of
hearts. Then there would have been no insult for the servants
of God—if, however, they were that—who received such a
quantity of goods from a woman they did not know, another
man's wife, in the absence and without the knowledge of her
husband. Then God would have been praised in your works,
which would have been accomplished in such trustful partnership that not only the most perfect chastity, but even glorious
poverty, would have been observed by you jointly.

But now see what you have done by your ill-advised haste.
For, although I should think charitably about those monks by
whom he complains that you were not edified, but robbed, and
should not readily side with a man whose eye is troubled
through indignation[45] against those who were perhaps servants of God, was the good you did in refreshing the bodies of
the poor by too lavish alms as great as the evil by which you
turned the mind of your husband from so good a purpose? Or
should the temporal welfare of anyone be dearer to you than
his eternal welfare? If, on considering the wider aspect of
mercy, you had postponed the distribution of your goods to
the poor to avoid being a stumbling-block to your husband,
thereby causing him to be lost to God, would not God have
credited you with more abundant alms? Besides, if you recall
what you gained when you won your husband to the service of
Christ in a holier chastity with you, understand what a grave
loss you suffered through that almsgiving of yours, a loss
greater than the heavenly gains of which you dreamed. For, if
the breaking of bread to the hungry[46] has such consideration
here, how much more must we believe there is for the mercy
by which a man is rescued from the devil, going about like a
raging lion seeking whom he may devour![47]

However, when I say this, I do not mean that if our good
works prove a stumbling-block to anyone we should think of
leaving them off. The case of strangers is different from the

45. Ps 6.8.   46. Is 58.7.
47. 1 Pt 5.8.

case of persons bound to us by any tie; the case of believers is not the same as that of unbelievers; the case of parents toward children differs from that of children toward parents; and, finally, the case of husband and wife (which is the one especially considered in the present circumstances) differs from the others, and the married woman has no right to say: "I do what I please with my own property," since she does not belong to herself, but to her head, that is, her husband.[48] For "after this manner," as the Apostle Peter says, "certain holy women who trusted in God adorned themselves, being in subjection to their own husbands; as Sara obeyed Abraham, calling him lord, whose daughters" he says "you are,"[49] and he was speaking to Christian, not to Jewish, women.

And what wonder that a father did not wish the son of both of you to be stripped of his means of support in this life, not knowing what state of life he would follow when he began to be a little older, whether it would be the profession of a monk or the ministry of the Church or the obligation of the married state? For, although the children of holy parents should be encouraged and trained for better things, "every one has his proper gift from God, one after this manner, another after that,"[50] unless, perhaps, a father is to be blamed for showing foresight and caution in such matters, although the blessed Apostle says: "If any man have not care of his own and especially of those of his house, he denies the faith and is worse than an infidel."[51] But when he spoke of almsgiving itself he said: "Not that others should be eased and you burdened."[52] Therefore you should have taken counsel together about everything; together you should have regulated what treasure is to be laid up in heaven and what is to be left as a means of support for yourselves, your dependents, and your son, so that other men be not eased and you burdened. In making and carrying out these arrangements, if any better plan happened to occur to you, you should have suggested it respectfully to your husband and bowed obediently to his authority as that of your head. In this way all who prize common sense, whom the news

48. Eph 5.23.
50. 1 Cor 7.7.
52. 2 Cor 8.13.
49. 1 Pt 3.5–6 and Gn 18.12.
51. 1 Tm 5.8.

of this good way of life could reach, would rejoice at the fruit-fulness and the peace of your household, and your enemy would be turned back, having nothing evil to say of you.

Moreover, if in the matter of almsgiving and bestowing your property on the poor, a good and great work about which we have precise commandments from the Lord, you ought to have taken counsel with your husband, a believer, and one who was observing with you the holy vow of continence, and not to have scorned his will, how much more necessary was it for you not to change or adopt anything in your costume and garb against his will—a matter on which we read no divine commands! It is true we read that women should appear in decent apparel and that the wearing of gold and the plaiting of hair[53] and other things of the kind which are usually put on either for idle display or to add allurement to beauty are deservedly reproved. But there is a certain matronly costume, appropriate to one's position in life, distinct from the widow's garb, which may be fitting for married women of the faith and which does not offend religious decorum. If your husband did not want you to lay this aside so that you might not flaunt yourself as a widow[54] during his lifetime, I think he should not have been driven to the scandal of a quarrel with you, with the result of more harm from your disobedience than good from any act of self-denial. For, what is more incongruous than for a woman to act haughtily toward her husband about a humble dress, when it would have been more profitable for you to display beauty in your conduct to him rather than stand out against him in a matter of mourning garb? Even if it had been a nun's dress that attracted you, could you not have assumed it with better grace if you had submitted to your husband and received his permission than you showed in presuming to put on widow's dress without consulting him or deferring to him? And if he absolutely refused his permission, how would your purpose have suffered? Perish the thought that God should be displeased at

---

53. 1 Tm 2.9 and 1 Pt 3.3.

54. This was a special dress of dark color, not unlike a religious habit, which distinguished widows, and was often conferred by the bishop. These women lived a retired and religious life and performed many charitable works for the Church.

your wearing, in your husband's lifetime, the dress, not of Anna[55] but of Susanna.[56]

But, if he who had begun with you to prize the great good of continence had wished you to wear the dress of a wife, not a widow, he would not thereby have obliged you to put on an unbecoming adornment, and, even if he had forced you to it by some harsh requirement, you could still have retained a humble heart under proud attire. Surely, in the time of the patriarchs the great Queen Esther feared God, worshipped God, and served God, yet she was submissive to her husband, a foreign king, who did not worship the same God as she did. And at a time of extreme danger not only to herself but to her race, the chosen people of God, she prostrated herself before God in prayer, and in her prayer she said that she regarded her royal attire as a menstruous rag,[57] and God "who sees the heart"[58] heard her prayer at once because He knew that she spoke the truth. But as for you, if your husband had remained steadfast in the plan of life he had undertaken with you, and had not rushed into sin because he was offended by you, you had in him a husband who was not only a believer and a wor-shiper with you of the true God, but even a man of continence who was certainly not unmindful of your joint resolution, and who would not have forced you to deck yourself with the or-naments of vanity even though he obliged you to wear the garb of a matron.

As you have seen fit to consult me, I have written this, not with the intent to break down your virtuous resolution by my words, but because I am grieved at your husband's conduct which is the result of your reckless and ill-considered behavior. You must now think very seriously about reclaiming him if you truly want to belong to Christ. Clothe yourself with lowliness of mind and, that God may keep you in constancy, do not scorn your husband in his fall. Pour out devout and continuous pray-ers for him, offer a sacrifice of tears as if it were the blood of a pierced heart, write him your apology, begging pardon for

55. The prophetess of Lk 2.36–38, a type of holy widowhood.

56. Cf. Dn 13.1–63. She was a type of chaste matron. St. Ambrose praises both women in *De. Vid.* 4.21–25.

57. Est 14.16.   58. Prv 21.12.

the sin you committed against him by disposing of your property according to what you thought should be done with it,
without asking his advice and consent; not that you should repent of having given it to the poor, but of having refused to let
him share and direct your good deed. Promise for the future,
with the Lord's help, that if he will repent of his shameful conduct and resume the continence which he has abandoned, you
will be subject to him in all things as it befits you to be: "If
peradventure God may give him repentance and he may re-
cover himself from the snares of the devil by whom he is held
captive at his will."[59] As for your son, since you brought him
forth in lawful and honorable wedlock, who does not know that
he is more subject to his father's authority than to yours?
Therefore, his father cannot be denied custody of him whenever he learns where he is and makes a legal demand for him.
Consequently, your union of hearts is necessary for him, also,
that he may be reared and trained in the wisdom of God.

59. Cf. 1 Tm 2.25–26.

MARRIAGE AND SEXUALITY IN
AUGUSTINE'S ANTI-MANICHEAN WRITINGS

For about nine years of his life, Augustine belonged to the Manichean "Auditors."[1] Although the higher rank within the Manicheans' religious stratification, the Elect, were forbidden to marry or reproduce, Auditors were allowed to marry or have concubines if they tried to prevent conception from occurring by various contraceptive techniques and sexual practices. For the Manicheans, reproduction served to further entrap the particles of Light that had been dispersed into the material world after the initial defeat of the power of Light by that of Darkness. Since our physical bodies were products of the power of Darkness that prevented the Light from returning to its heavenly home, the Manicheans believed that procreation was an evil. After his conversion to Christianity, Augustine faulted the Manichean notion that our bodies are the products of an evil power and that reproduction is a ploy of the power of Darkness. In opposition to the Manicheans, Augustine came to champion a sexual ethic for married couples that was pro-reproductive and anti-contraceptive. In the following passages, Augustine criticizes the Manichean notion of creation and the ethical consequences derived from it.

Some sections of Augustine's treatise On Continence, *composed*

1. For a good history of Manicheanism, see Samuel N.C. Lieu, *Manichaeism in the Later Roman Empire and Medieval China*. 2nd ed. (Tübingen: J.C.B. Mohr, 1992).

probably after 412, are directed against Manichean sexual ethics. At the root of their erroneous views, Augustine suggests, is the heretical view that our bodies are evil:[2]

CHAPTER 9

(22) By what error, therefore, not error but rather madness—do the Manichaeans attribute our flesh to some fabulous race of darkness which they claim has always held its evil nature without any beginning, when that truthful Doctor[3] urges husbands to love their wives, giving the example of their own flesh, whom he exhorts to be same thing also by the example of Christ and His Church? The entire passage of the apostolic Epistle, exceedingly pertinent here, ought to be quoted: "Husbands," he says, "love your wives, just as Christ also loved the Church, and delivered Himself up for her, that He might sanctify her, cleansing her in the bath of water by means of the word; in order that He might present to Himself the Church in all her glory, not having spot or wrinkle, or any such thing, but that she might be holy and without blemish. Even thus," he says, "ought husbands also to love their wives as their own bodies. He who loves his own wife, loves himself." Then he added what we have mentioned just above: "For no one ever hated his own flesh; on the contrary he nourishes and cherishes it, as Christ also does the Church."[4] What does the madness of foulest impiety say to this? What do you say to this, you Manichaeans, you who attempt to bring forward to us, indeed as if from the apostolic Epistles, two natures without beginning, one of good and the other of evil; and the apostolic Epistles, which correct you from that sacrilegious perversity of yours, you do not want to hear. Just as you read: "the flesh lusts against the spirit,"[5] and: "In my flesh no good dwells,"[6] so also read: "No one ever hated his own flesh, but nourishes and cherishes it, as also Christ does the Church."[7] And as you read: "I see another law in my members warring against the law of my mind,"[8] so also read this: "As Christ loved the Church, so also ought men to

2. FOTC 16.215–216.   3. Paul.
4. Eph 5.25–29.   5. Gal 5.17.
6. Rom 7.18.   7. Eph 5.29.
8. Rom 7.23.

love their wives as their own bodies."[9] Do not be crafty in using the one group of testimonies of sacred Scripture and deaf to the other, and you will be corrected in both. For, if you accept these latter as they deserve, you will try to understand the former, also, in their truth.

Because of their belief that the body was evil, some Manicheans adopted lives of sexual continence. According to Augustine, however, theirs was a false restraint because it was motivated by erroneous beliefs about the value of the body and the power who had created it. Continence, for Augustine, must always be motivated by love for God and must always be understood as God's gift. Thus he writes in his treatise On Continence:[10]

CHAPTER 12

(26) It will be sufficient to have mentioned these points in behalf of true continence against the Manichaeans who are deceitfully continent, lest the fruitful and glorious labor of continence when it checks and restrains our weak part, that is, the body, from immoderate and unlawful pleasures be considered not to healthfully chastise us, but to hostilely assault. The body is by nature certainly opposed to the soul, but it is not alien to the nature of man. The soul is not made up of the body, but man is made up of soul and body, and, surely, whom God sets free He sets free as a whole man. Whence, the Savior Himself assumed a whole human nature, deigning to free in us the whole that He had made. As for those who hold opinions contrary to this truth, of what advantage is it for them to restrain the passions, if, however, they do restrain any? What can be made clean by continence in them whose continence is such an unclean thing and which ought not to be called continence? In truth, what they feel should be held is the poison of the Devil, whereas continence is a gift of God .... [N]ot everyone who restrains something, or even one who restrains the very delights of the flesh or mind in a marvelous manner, must be said to possess that continence whose utility and beauty we have been discussing. Certain people, and it may seem strange to

say this, restrain themselves through incontinence, for example, if a woman should withhold herself from intercourse with her husband because she had conspired in this with an adulterer. Some restrain themselves through injustice, as is the case when one spouse does not render to the other the debt of intercourse, because the one or the other can already overcome such an appetite of the flesh. Further some "are continent," deceived by false faith, both putting trust in vanities and pursuing vanities. Among this number are all heretics and those who are deceived by any error under the name of religion. The continence of such people would be true if their faith also were true; but, because of the fact that the one ought not to be given the name of "faith," because it is false, without doubt neither is the other worthy of the name of "continence." Are we saying, then, that the continence which we speak of most truly as a gift of God is a sin? Far from our hearts be such detestable madness! The blessed Apostle, though, says: "All that is not from faith is sin."[11] That, therefore, which does not have faith should not be named continence.

Some Manicheans, Augustine alleges, not only commit sexual sins, but they also try to excuse themselves by claiming that the power of evil was stronger than the power of God:[12]

CHAPTER 5

(14) . . . And there are also some[13] who extend their excuse into an accusation of God. These are wretched by the judgment of God, but they are blasphemers by their own fury. For, against Him, from a contrary principle, they concoct a rebellious substance of evil, which He could not have resisted unless He had mingled with that same rebellious substance a part of His own nature and substance, thereby contaminating and corrupting it. Then they sin, they say, whenever the nature of evil prevails over the nature of God. This is that most foul madness of the Manichaeans, whose diabolical machinations are very

11. Rom 14.23.   12. FOTC 16.205.
13. At this point St. Augustine begins his revelation of the Manichaean attitude toward the flesh as not continence but the worst uncleanness.

easily overcome by the unquestionable truth which confesses the incontaminable and incorruptible nature of God. On the other hand, what depth of wicked contamination and corruption may we not rightly impute to those by whom God, who is supremely and incomparably good, is believed to be contaminable and corruptible?

He provides an example of the bad sexual behavior of some Manicheans:[14]

CHAPTER 12

(27) There are also some who are "continent" from the desires of the body in open service to the spirits of evil, that through them they might satisfy base desires, the impetus and ardor of which they do not restrain. To mention an instance and pass by the rest in silence because of the length of this discussion[15]—some do not even touch their own wives, and while clean, as it were, they endeavor through the arts of magic to approach unto the wives of others. Strange continence! Rather, indeed, singular evil and uncleanness! For, if this were true continence, the concupiscence of the flesh ought to withhold from marriage rather than from adultery for the perpetration of adultery! Conjugal continence, indeed, usually abates the concupiscence of the flesh and imposes moderation on its reins only to such an extent that in the marriage itself it is not poured out in unmoderated license, but that measure is observed, either that owed to the weakness of the spouse to whom the Apostle does not charge it by commandment but to whom he yields it by indulgence,[16] or that suited to the procreation of children, which was in the past the only cause of sexual intercourse for holy fathers and mothers. But, when continence does this, that is, when it moderates and in a certain way limits the concupiscence of the flesh in married people and ordains its restless and inordinate motion, in a manner, to cer-

14. FOTC 16.224–225.
15. The term St. Augustine uses is *sermo,* but it need not be taken in the restricted English sense of sermon. His DME (PL 32.1345–1378) goes into greater detail on the habits and manner of this sect.)
16. Cf. 1 Cor 7.6.

tain ends, it uses in a good way the evil of man whom it makes and wants to make thoroughly good; just as God uses evil men also for the sake of those whom He perfects in good.

When Augustine countered Manichean charges that Genesis accounts were too "earthy," unbefitting the edification of a truly religious person, he tended to champion an allegorical, "spiritualized" exegesis of Genesis 1.28. Later, he was to reject such allegory in favor of a more literal—and "physical"—reading. But in On Genesis, Against the Manichees, *dating to 388–89, he writes as follows:*[17]

BOOK ONE, CHAPTER 19

30. There follows the words, "He made them male and female, and God blessed them, saying, 'Increase and multiply, and generate and fill the earth.'"[18] Here one is completely right to ask in what sense we should understand the union of the male and female before sin, as well as the blessing that said, "Increase and multiply, and generate and fill the earth." Should we understand it carnally or spiritually? For we are permitted to understand it spiritually and to believe that it was changed into carnal fecundity after sin.[19] For there was first the chaste

17. FOTC 84.77–78, 111–112, 114–115, and 123–124.
18. Gn 1.27–28.
19. In R 1.10.2 Augustine says, "One reads [in DGnM] that we should believe that the blessing of God by which he said, 'Increase and multiply,' was changed into carnal fecundity after the sin. If this cannot be understood otherwise than as saying that those humans would not have children if they had not sinned, I completely disapprove." In DVR 46.88 Augustine says that "we would not have any such temporal relationships which arise by being born or dying, if our nature remained in the precepts and image of God and was not dismissed to this corruption." And of that passage he says in R 1.13.8, "I completely disapprove of this meaning which I already rejected above in the first book of *On Genesis against the Manichees.* For it leads to the belief that the first spouses would not have generated later humans if they had not sinned, as if it were necessary that they be born destined to die, if they were born from the relations of husband and wife. For I had not yet seen that it was possible that offspring not destined to die would be born from parents not destined to die, if human nature were not changed for the worse by that great sin. In this way, if fecundity and felicity had remained in both parents and offspring until the certain number of the saints which 'God has predestined' (cf. Rom 8.28ff., 1 Cor 2.7, and Eph 1.5, 11), men would be born not to take the place of dying

union of male and female, of the former to rule, of the latter to obey, and there was the spiritual offspring of intelligible and immortal joys filling the earth, that is, giving life to the body and ruling it. That is, man so held [the body] subject that he experienced from it no opposition or trouble. We should believe that it was this way, since they were not yet children of this world before they sinned. For the children of this world generate and are generated, as the Lord says, when he shows that we should condemn this carnal generation in comparison with the future life which is promised us.[20]

BOOK TWO, CHAPTER 13

18. As the master, the man gave a name to his woman, his inferior, and said, "Now this is bone from my bones, and flesh from my flesh."[21] "Bone from my bones" perhaps on account of fortitude. "Flesh from my flesh" on account of temperance. For these two virtues, we are taught, pertain to the lower part of the mind that the prudence of reason rules.[22] It said, "She will be called woman because she was taken from her man."[23] This derivation and interpretation of the name is not apparent in the Latin language. For we do not find any similarity between the word, "woman" *(mulier)*, and the word, "man" *(vir)*. But in the Hebrew language the expression is said to sound just as if one said: "She is called a *virago* because she was taken from her *vir.*" For *virago* or rather *virgo* has some similarity with the word, *vir,* while *mulier* does not, but this is caused by the difference of languages.[24]

---

parents, but to reign with living ones. Hence, there would be these relationships and ties even if no one sinned and no one died."

20. Lk 20.34–36. The Latin is ambiguous as to whether Augustine has the Lord teaching us to contemn the act of generating carnally or the carnal generation in which we live. Both meanings, of course, are probably intended.

21. Gn 2.23.

22. This doctrine is found in Aristotle's *Nichomachean Ethics* 1102a28–1102b34, though Augustine probably learned it from a Latin author, such as Cicero; cf. *De Officiis* 1.102–103.

23. Gn 2.23.

24. In Hebrew the terms, "man" and "woman," are ʾish and ʾishah. There is no such similarity between the Latin, *vir* and *mulier. Virago* means "man-like woman" or "female warrior," and *virgo* means "maiden." Both are derived from *vir.* The Vulgate has *virago.*

19. Scripture said, "A man will leave father and mother and he will cling to his wife, and they will be two in one flesh."[25] I find no way that this pertains to history except insofar as this is what generally happens in the human race.[26] Rather this is all prophecy, and the Apostle reminds us of this when he says, "For this reason a man will leave his father and mother and he will cling to his wife, and they will be two in one flesh. This is a great mystery; I mean in Christ and in the Church."[27] If the Manichees who deceive many by means of the Letters of the Apostle did not read this blindly, they would understand how to interpret the Scriptures of the Old Testament, and they would not dare to bring charges with such sacrilegious words against what they do not understand. The fact that Adam and his wife "were naked and were not embarrassed"[28] signifies simplicity and chastity of soul. For the Apostle speaks this way: "I have joined you to one husband to present to Christ a chaste virgin; but I fear lest, as the serpent deceived Eve by his cleverness, so your minds may be corrupted from the simplicity and chastity which is in Christ."[29]

BOOK TWO, CHAPTER 11

15 . . . Hence, Scripture begins to explain how the woman was made. It says that she was made as man's helper so that by spiritual union she might bring forth spiritual offspring, that is, the good works of divine praise, while he rules and she obeys. He is ruled by wisdom, she by the man. For Christ is the head of the man, and the man is the head of the woman.[30] Thus it said, "It is not good that man is alone."[31] For there was still need to bring it about not only that the soul rule over the body, because the body has the position of a servant, but also that virile reason hold subject to itself its animal part, by the help of which it governs the body. The woman was made as an illustration of this, for the order of things makes her subject to

25. Gn 2.24.
26. Since leaving one's parents cannot be taken according to history in Adam's case, it either refers to what generally happens in the human race or is a mystery that signifies the union of Christ and the Church.

27. Eph 5.31–32.   28. Cf. Gn 2.25.
29. 2 Cor 11.2–3.   30. Cf. 1 Cor 11.3.
31. Gn 2.18.

man. Thus we can also come to see in one human what we can see more clearly in two humans, that is, in the male and the female. The interior mind, like virile reason, should hold subject the soul's appetite by means of which we control the members of the body, and by just law it should place a limit upon its helper, just as man ought to rule woman and ought not to allow her to rule him. When this happens, the home is perverted and unhappy.

BOOK TWO, CHAPTER 19

29. There is no question about the punishment of the woman. For she clearly has her pains and sighs multiplied in the woes of this life.[32] Although her bearing her children in pain is fulfilled in this visible woman, our consideration should nevertheless be recalled to that more hidden woman. For even in animals the females bear offspring with pain, and this is in their case the condition of mortality rather than the punishment of sin. Hence, it is possible that this be the condition of mortal bodies even in the females of humans. But this is the great punishment: they have come to the present bodily mortality from their former immortality.[33] Still there is a great mystery in this sentence, because there is no restraint from carnal desire which does not have pain in the beginning, until habit has been bent toward the better part. When this has come about, it is as though a child is born, that is, the good habit disposes our intentions toward the good deed. In order that this habit might be born, there was a painful struggle with bad habit.[34] Scripture adds after the birth, "You will turn to your man, and he will rule over you."[35] Do not many or almost all women give birth while their husbands are absent and, after the birth, turn to them? There are, of course, proud women

32. Cf. Gn 3.16.

33. Though Augustine does not have an Aristotelian concept of nature, without which the concepts of supernatural and preternatural cannot be clearly defined, there is present here an adumbration of the doctrine that the immortality of the first parents was a preternatural gift. That is, it could be natural for women to bear children in pain; the penal aspect is the loss of the previous immortality.

34. Augustine compares habits to chains; cf. C 8.5.10.

35. Gn 3.16.

who rule their men. Do they lack this vice after giving birth so that their husbands rule them? No, indeed! They even believe that they have acquired a dignity by becoming mothers and they generally emerge as even more proud. After saying, "You will bear your children in pain," it adds, "and your turning will be to your husband, and he will rule over you." What can this mean except that, when that part of the soul held by carnal joys has, in willing to conquer a bad habit, suffered difficulty and pain and in this way brought forth a good habit, it now more carefully and diligently obeys reason as its husband? And, taught by its pains, it turns to reason and willingly obeys its commands lest it again decline to some harmful habit. Hence, those things which seemed to be curses are commandments, if we do not read those spiritual things in a carnal way. For the Law is spiritual.[36]

Before too many years had passed, Augustine came to realize that, although his spiritualized reading of Genesis 1–2 provided a useful interpretive strategy when he confronted Manicheans, it laid him open to charges that he had espoused an overly-ascetic sexual ethic. In the early 400's, Augustine began to compose treatises that pronounced his blessing on marriage and reproduction in all their physicality and that gave a more literal, "material" interpretation of the Biblical creation story. Nonetheless, later in life, Augustine's linking of sexual desire to the first sin prompted his Pelagian opponents to claim that he was still a covert Manichean. These developments, and Augustine's responses, are the subject of the next two chapters.

36. Cf. Rom 7.14.

3

THE ASCETIC DEBATES AND
AUGUSTINE'S RESPONSE

*During the course of the 380s, the ascetic movement gained ground
in Western Christianity. Its prime advocate was Jerome, who during his
sojourn at Rome in the early 380s encouraged aristocratic women to
adopt lives of celibacy.[1] Not only pagans, but many Christians as well,
thought that Jerome's exaltation of virginity implied a denigration of
marriage.[2] Jerome's ascetic views received such criticism that he left
Rome for Palestine in 385, from whence he continued his advocacy of
the celibate life for Christians.*

*In the early 390s, Jerome composed a refutation of a Christian
writer named Jovinian who had extolled the goodness of marriage,
claiming that it was equal in status with virginity if the married person
led a virtuous life in other respects. He argued that writers such as
Jerome praised ascetic renunciation so excessively that they veered toward a Manichean denigration of the body and reproduction. Jerome
in his response,* Against Jovinian, *made clear that he indeed did think
that marriage was a lower way of life than celibacy, although he hotly
denied that his view was "Manichean."*

1. For a discussion, see J.N.D. Kelly, *Jerome* (London: Duckworth Press, 1975).

2. For the issues involved, see David G. Hunter, "Resistance to the Virginal
Ideal in Late-Fourth-Century Rome: The Case of Jovinian," *Theological Studies*
48 (1987) 45–64; S. D. Driver, "The Development of Jerome's Views on the
Ascetic Life," *RTAM* 62 (1995) 44–70.

When Augustine in North Africa learned of the dispute between Jerome and Jovinian several years after the fact, he was troubled. In response, he composed treatises that struck a middle ground in the debate, one that conceded the superiority of virginity but nonetheless upheld the goodness of marriage more adequately than had Jerome. Around 401, Augustine wrote two treatises addressing these issues. Many of the Scriptural passages he cites therein were ones that Jerome and Jovinian had used in their respective arguments. The first of these treatises, The Good of Marriage, *expresses a view of the subject that has largely prevailed in Catholic teaching ever since. Augustine writes as follows in* The Good of Marriage:[3]

CHAPTER 1

Since every man is a part of the human race, and human nature is something social and possesses the capacity for friendship as a great and natural good, for this reason God wished to create all men from one, so that they might be held together in their society, not only by the similarity of race, but also by the bond of blood relationship. And so it is that the first natural tie of human society is man and wife. Even these God did not create separately and join them as if strangers, but He made the one from the other, indicating also the power of union in the side from where she was drawn and formed.[4] They are joined to each other side by side who walk together and observe together where they are walking. A consequence is the union of society in the children who are the only worthy fruit, not of the joining of male and female, but of sexual intercourse. For there could have been in both sexes, even without such intercourse, a kind of friendly and genuine union of the one ruling and the other obeying.

CHAPTER 2

(2) There is no need now for us to examine and put forth a final opinion on this question—how the progeny of the first parents might have come into being, whom God had blessed, saying, "Be fruitful and multiply; fill the earth,"[5] if they had not sinned, since their bodies deserved the condition of death

---

3. FOTC 27.9–14, 16–27, 30–31, 39, 42–44, 47, 49–51, *passim*.
4. Cf. Gn 2.21.   5. Gn 1.28.

by sinning, and there could not be intercourse except of mortal bodies. Many different opinions have existed on this subject, and, if we must examine which of them agrees most with the truth of divine Scriptures, there is matter for an extended discussion:[6] Whether, for example, if our first parents had not sinned, they would have had children in some other way, without physical coition, out of the munificence of the almighty Creator, who was able to create them without parents, and who was able to form the body of Christ in a virgin's womb, and who, to speak now to the unbelievers themselves, was able to grant progeny to bees without intercourse; whether, in that passage, much was spoken in a mystical and figurative sense and the written words are to be understood differently: "Fill the earth and subdue it," that is, that it should come to pass by the fullness and the perfection of life and power that the increasing and multiplying, where it is said: "Be fruitful and multiply," might be understood to be by the advancement of the mind and by the fullness of virtue, as it is expressed in the psalm: "You will multiply me in my soul unto virtue,"[7] and that succession of offspring was not granted to man except that later, because of sin, there was to be a departure in death; whether, at first, the body of those men had been made spiritual but animal, so that afterwards by the merit of obedience it might become spiritual to grasp immortality, not after death, which came into the world through the envy of the Devil[8] and became the punishment for sin, but through that change which the Apostle indicates where he says: "Then we who live, who survive, shall be caught up together with them in clouds to meet the Lord in the air,"[9] so that we may understand that the bodies of the first marriage were both mortal at the first formation and yet would not have died, if they had not sinned, as God had threatened,[10] just as if He threatened a wound, because the body was vulnerable, which, however, would not have happened, unless that was done which He had forbidden.

Thus, then, even through sexual intercourse generations of such bodies could have come into existence, which would have

6. Cf. DCD 1.14.   7. Cf. Ps 137(138).3.
8. Cf. Wis 2.24.   9. 1 Thes 4.17.
10. Cf. Gn 2.17.

had increase up to a certain point and yet would not have inclined to old age, or they would have inclined as far as old age and yet not to death, until the earth should be filled with that multiplication of the blessing. For, if God granted to the garments of the Israelites[11] their proper state without any damage for forty years, how much more would He have granted a very happy temperament of certain state to the bodies of those who obeyed His command, until they would be turned into something better, not by the death of man, by which the body is deserted by the soul, but by a blessed change from mortality to immortality, from an animal to a spiritual quality.

CHAPTER 3

It would be tedious to inquire and to discuss which of these opinions is true, or whether another or other opinions can still be extracted from these words.

(3) This is what we now say, that according to the present condition of birth and death, which we know and in which we were created, the marriage of male and female is something good. This union divine Scripture so commands that it is not permitted a woman who has been dismissed by her husband to marry again, as long as her husband lives, nor is it permitted a man who has been dismissed by his wife to marry again, unless she who left has died. Therefore, regarding the good of marriage, which even the Lord confirmed in the Gospel,[12] not only because He forbade the dismissal of a wife except for fornication, but also because He came to the marriage when invited,[13] there is merit in inquiring why it is a good.

This does not seem to me to be a good solely because of the procreation of children, but also because of the natural companionship between the two sexes. Otherwise, we could not speak of marriage in the case of old people, especially if they had either lost their children or had begotten none at all. But, in a good marriage, although one of many years, even if the ardor of youth has cooled between man and woman, the order of charity still flourishes between husband and wife. They are better in proportion as they begin the earlier to refrain by mu-

11. Cf. Dt 29.5.   12. Cf. Mt 19.9.
13. Cf. Jn 2.

tual consent from sexual intercourse, not that it would afterwards happen of necessity that they would not be able to do
what they wished, but that it would be a matter of praise that
they had refused beforehand what they were able to do. Sup-
pose, then, that the promise of respect and of services due to
the other by either sex is observed. In that case, even though
both members weaken in health and become almost corpse-
like, chastity, that of souls rightly joined together, continues—
and it becomes more pure, the more it has been proved, and
more secure, the more it has been calmed.

Marriage has also this good, that carnal or youthful incontinence, even if it is bad, is turned to the honorable task of begetting children, so that marital intercourse makes something
good out of the evil of lust. Finally, the concupiscence of the
flesh, which parental affection tempers, is repressed and becomes inflamed more modestly. For a kind of dignity prevails
when, as husband and wife they unite in the marriage act, they
think of themselves as mother and father.

CHAPTER 4

(4) There is the added fact that, in the very debt which married persons owe each other, even if they demand its payment
somewhat intemperately and incontinently, they owe fidelity
equally to each other. And to this fidelity the Apostle has attributed so much right that he called it authority, when he said:
"The wife has not authority over her body, but the husband;
the husband likewise has not authority over his body, but the
wife."[14] But the violation of this fidelity is called adultery, when,
either by the instigation of one's own lust or by consent to the
lust of another, there is intercourse with another contrary to
the marriage compact. And so the fidelity is broken which even
in material and base things is a great good of the soul; and so
it is certain that it ought to be preferred even to the health of
the body wherein his life is contained. For, although a small
amount of straw as compared to much gold is as nothing, fidelity, when it is kept pure in a matter of straw, as in a matter
of gold, is not of less importance on this account because it is
kept in a matter of less value.

14. 1 Cor 7.4.

But, when fidelity is employed to commit sin, we wonder whether it ought to be called fidelity. However, whatever its nature may be, if even against this something is done, it has an added malice; except when this is abandoned with the view that there might be a return to the true and lawful fidelity, that is, that the sin might be amended by correcting the depravity of the will.

For example, if anyone, when he is unable to rob a man by himself, finds an accomplice for his crime and makes an agreement with him to perform the act together and share the loot, and, after the crime has been committed, he runs off with everything, the other naturally grieves and complains that fidelity had not been observed in his regard. In his very complaint he ought to consider that he should have observed his fidelity to human society by means of a good life, so that he would not rob a man unjustly, if he feels how wickedly fidelity was not kept with him in an association of sin. His partner, faithless on both counts, is certainly to be judged the more wicked. But, if he had been displeased with the wickedness which they had committed and so had refused to divide the spoils with his partner in crime on this account, that he could return them to the man from whom they were taken, not even the faithless man would call him faithless.

So, in the case of a woman who has broken her marriage fidelity but remains faithful to her adulterer, she is surely wicked, but, if she is not faithful even to her adulterer, she is worse. On the contrary, if she repents of her gross sin and returns to conjugal chastity and breaks off all adulterous unions and purposes, I cannot conceive of even the adulterer himself thinking of her as a violator of fidelity.

CHAPTER 6

There also are men incontinent to such a degree that they do not spare their wives even when pregnant. Whatever immodest, shameful, and sordid acts the married commit with each other are the sins of the married persons themselves, not the fault of marriage.

(6) Furthermore, in the more immoderate demand of the carnal debt, which the Apostle enjoined on them not as a command but conceded as a favor, to have sexual intercourse even

without the purpose of procreation, although evil habits impel them to such intercourse, marriage protects them from adultery and fornication. For this is not permitted because of the marriage, but because of the marriage it is pardoned. Therefore, married people owe each other not only the fidelity of sexual intercourse for the purpose of procreating children—and this is the first association of the human race in this mortal life—but also the mutual service, in a certain measure, of sustaining each other's weakness, for the avoidance of illicit intercourse, so that, even if perpetual continence is pleasing to one of them, he may not follow this urge except with the consent of the other. In this case, "The wife has not authority over her body, but the husband; the husband likewise has not authority over his body, but the wife." So, let them not deny either to each other, what the man seeks from matrimony and the woman from her husband, not for the sake of having children but because of weakness and incontinence, lest in this way they fall into damnable seductions through the temptations of Satan because of the incontinence of both or of one of them.

In marriage, intercourse for the purpose of generation has no fault attached to it, but for the purpose of satisfying concupiscence, provided with a spouse, because of the marriage fidelity, it is a venial sin; adultery or fornication, however, is a mortal sin. And so, continence from all intercourse is certainly better than marital intercourse itself which takes place for the sake of begetting children.

CHAPTER 7

While continence is of greater merit, it is no sin to render the conjugal debt, but to exact it beyond the need for generation is a venial sin; furthermore, to commit fornication or adultery is a crime that must be punished. Conjugal charity should be on its guard lest, while it seeks for itself the means of being honored more, it creates for the spouse the means of damnation. "Everyone who puts away his wife, save on account of immorality, causes her to commit adultery."[15] To such a degree is that nuptial pact which has been entered upon a kind of sacrament that it is not nullified by separation, since, as long as

15. Mt 5.32.

the husband, by whom she has been abandoned, is alive, she commits adultery if she marries another, and he who abandoned her is the cause of the evil.

(7) I wonder if, as it is permitted to put away an adulterous wife, it is accordingly permitted, after she has been put away, to marry another. Holy Scripture creates a difficult problem in this matter, since the Apostle says[16] that according to the command of the Lord a wife is not to depart from her husband, but, if she departs, she ought to remain unmarried or be reconciled to her husband. She surely ought not to withdraw and remain unmarried except in the case of an adulterous husband, lest, by withdrawing from him who is not an adulterer, she causes him to commit adultery. But, perhaps she can justly be reconciled with her husband either by tolerating him, if she on her own part cannot contain herself, or after he has been corrected. But I do not see how a man can have freedom to marry another if he leaves an adulteress, since a woman does not have freedom to marry another if she leaves an adulterer.

If this is so, that bond of fellowship between married couples is so strong that, although it is tied for the purpose of procreation, it is not loosed for the purpose of procreation. For, a man might be able to dismiss a wife who is barren and marry someone by whom he might have children, yet in our times and according to Roman law it is not permissible to marry a second wife as long as he has another wife living. Surely, when an adulteress or adulterer is abandoned, more human beings could be born if either the woman were wed to another or the man married another. But, if this is not permitted, as divine Law seems to prescribe, who will not be eager to learn what the meaning of such a strong conjugal bond is? I do not think that this bond could by any means have been so strong, unless a symbol, as it were, of something greater than that which could arise from our weak mortality were applied, something that would remain unshaken for the punishment of men when they abandon and attempt to dissolve this bond, inasmuch as, when divorce intervenes, that nuptial contract is not destroyed, so that the parties of the compact are wedded persons even though separated.

16. Cf. 1 Cor 7.10–11.

Moreover, they commit adultery with those with whom they have intercourse even after their repudiation, whether she with a man, or he with a woman. Yet, except "in the city of our God, His holy mountain,"[17] such is not the case with a woman.

CHAPTER 8

But who does not know that the laws of the pagans are otherwise. Among them, when repudiation intervenes, both she marries whomever she wishes and he whomever he wishes, without any offense that requires human punishment. Moses, because of the Israelites' hardness of heart,[18] seems to have permitted something similar to this practice regarding a written notice of dismissal.[19] In this matter there appears to be a rebuke rather than an approval of divorce.

(8) "Let marriage be held in honor with all, and let the marriage bed be undefiled."[20] We do not call marriage a good in this sense, that in comparison with fornication it is a good; otherwise, there will be two evils, one of which is worse. Or even fornication will be a good because adultery is worse—since violation of another's marriage is worse than associating with a prostitute. Or adultery will be a good because incest is worse since intercourse with one's mother is worse than living with another's wife—and so on, until we come to those things about which, as the Apostle says: "It is shameful even to speak."[21] All will be good in comparison with that which is worse. But who would doubt that this is false? Therefore, marriage and fornication are not two evils, the second of which is worse; but marriage and continence are two goods, the second of which is better. Just so, your temporal health and sickness are not two evils, the second of which is worse; but your health and immortality are two goods, the second of which is better. . . .

Therefore, just as that was good which Martha did when occupied with the ministering to holy souls, yet that was better which Mary her sister did, who "seated herself at the Lord's feet, and listened to his words";[22] so we praise the good of Susanna[23] in married chastity, yet we place above it the good

17. Ps 47(48).2.
18. Cf. Mt 19.8.
19. Cf. Dt 24.1.
20. Heb 13.4.
21. Eph 5.12.
22. Cf. Lk 10.39.
23. Dn 13.

of the widow Anna[24] and much more so that of the Virgin Mary.[25] That was good which they were doing who out of their substance were supplying the necessaries to Christ and His disciples, but they did better who gave away all their substance that they might follow the same Lord more readily. In both these goods, whether what the latter did or what Martha and Mary did, the better could not be done without passing over and abandoning the other.

We must understand that marriage is not to be considered an evil for this reason, that widowed chastity or virginal purity cannot be possessed unless there is abstinence from marriage. Nor was that which Martha did an evil for this reason, that, unless her sister abstained from it, she would not be doing what was better; nor is it an evil to take a just man or a prophet into one's house, because he who wishes to follow Christ unto perfection, in order that he might do what is better, ought not to own any house at all.

CHAPTER 9

(9) Surely we must see that God gives us some goods which are to be sought for their own sake, such as wisdom, health, friendship; others, which are necessary for something else, such as learning, food, drink, sleep, marriage, sexual intercourse. Certain of these are necessary for the sake of wisdom, such as learning; others for the sake of health, such as food and drink and sleep; others for the sake of friendship, such as marriage or intercourse, for from this comes the propagation of the human race in which friendly association is a great good. So, whoever does not use these goods, which are necessary for something else, for the purpose for which they are given does well. As for him for whom they are not necessary, if he does not use them, he does better. In like manner, we wish for these goods rightly when we have need, but we are better off not wishing for them than wishing for them, since we possess them in a better way when we possess them as not necessary.

For this reason it is a good to marry, since it is a good to beget children, to be the mother of a family; but it is better not to marry, since it is better for human society itself not to have

24. Cf. Lk 2.36.   25. Cf. Lk 1.28.

need of marriage. For, such is the present state of the human race that not only some who do not check themselves are taken up with marriage, but many are wanton and given over to illicit intercourse. Since the good Creator draws good out of their evils, there is no lack of numerous progeny and an abundance of generation whence holy friendships might be sought out.

In this regard it is gathered that in the earliest times of the human race, especially to propagate the people of God, through whom the Prince and Saviour of all peoples might both be prophesied and be born, the saints were obliged to make use of this good of marriage, to be sought not for its own sake but as necessary for something else. But now, since the opportunity for spiritual relationship abounds on all sides and for all peoples for entering into a holy and pure association, even they who wish to contract marriage only to have children are to be admonished that they practice the greater good of continence.

CHAPTER 10

(10) But I know what they murmur. "What if," they say, "all men should be willing to restrain themselves from all inter-course, how would the human race survive?" Would that all men had this wish, if only in "charity, from a pure heart and a good conscience and faith unfeigned."[26] Much more quickly would the City of God be filled and the end of time be has-tened. What else does it appear that the Apostle is encouraging when he says, in speaking of this: "For I would that you all were as I am myself"?[27] Or, in another place: "But this I say, breth-ren, the time is short; it remains that those who have wives be as if they had none; and those who weep, as though not weep-ing; and those who rejoice, as though not rejoicing; and those who buy, as though not buying; and those who use this world, as though not using it, for this world as we see it is passing away. I would have you free from care." Then he adds: "He who is unmarried thinks about the things of the Lord, how he may please the Lord. Whereas he who is married thinks about the things of the world, how he may please his wife, and he is di-vided. And the unmarried woman and the virgin, who is un-

<hr>

26. 1 Tm 1.5.   27. 1 Cor 7.7.

married, is concerned about the things of the Lord, that she may be holy in body and in spirit. Whereas she who is married is concerned about the things of the world, how she may please her husband."[28]

And so it seems to me that at this time only those who do not restrain themselves ought to be married in accord with this saying of the same Apostle: "But if they do not have self-control, let them marry, for it is better to marry than to burn."[29]

(11) Such marriage is not a sin. If it were chosen in preference to fornication, it would be a lesser sin than fornication, but still a sin. But now what are we to say in answer to that very clear statement of the Apostle when he says: "Let him do what he will; he does not sin if she should marry"[30] and "But if you take a wife, you have not sinned. And if a virgin marries, she does not sin."[31] Certainly from this it is not right to doubt that marriage is not a sin. And so it is not the marriage that the Apostle grants as a pardon—for who would doubt that it is most absurd to say that they have not sinned to whom a pardon is granted—but it is that sexual intercourse that comes about through incontinence, not for the sake of procreation and at the time with no thought of procreation, that he grants as a pardon. Marriage does not force this type of intercourse to come about, but asks that it be pardoned, provided it is not so great as to encroach on the times that ought to be set aside for prayer, and does not degenerate into that practice that is against nature, which the Apostle was not able to pass over in silence when he spoke of the extreme depravities of impure and impious men.[32]

The intercourse necessary for generation is without fault and it alone belongs to marriage. The intercourse that goes beyond this necessity no longer obeys reason but passion. Still, not to demand this intercourse but to render it to a spouse, lest he sin mortally by fornication, concerns the married person. But, if both are subject to such concupiscence, they do something that manifestly does not belong to marriage. However, if in their union they love what is proper rather than what is im-

28. 1 Cor 7.29–34.   29. 1 Cor 7.9.
30. 1 Cor 7.36.   31. 1 Cor 7.28.
32. Cf. Rom 1.26.

proper, that is, what belongs to marriage rather than that which does not, this is granted to them with the Apostle as an authority. They do not have a marriage that encourages this crime, but one that intercedes for them, if they do not turn away from themselves the mercy of God, either by not abstaining on certain days so as to be free for prayers, and by this abstinence as by their fasts they put their prayers in a favorable light, or by changing the natural use into that use which is contrary to nature, which is all the more damnable in a spouse.

CHAPTER 11

(12) For, although the natural use, when it goes beyond the marriage rights, that is, beyond the need for procreation, is pardonable in a wife but damnable in a prostitute, that use which is against nature is abominable in a prostitute but more abominable in a wife. For, the decree of the Creator and the right order of the creature are of such force that, even though there is an excess in the things that have been granted to be used, this is much more tolerable than a single or rare deviation in those things which have not been granted. Therefore, the immoderation of a spouse in a matter that is permitted is to be tolerated lest lust may break forth into something that has not been granted. So it is that, however demanding one is as regards his wife, he sins much less than one who commits fornication even most rarely.

But, when the husband wishes to use the member of his wife which has not been given for this purpose, the wife is more shameful if she permits this to take place with herself rather than with another woman. The crown of marriage, then, is the chastity of procreation and faithfulness in rendering the carnal debt. This is the province of marriage, this is what the Apostle defended from all blame by saying: "But if you take a wife, you have not sinned. And if a virgin marries, she does not sin"[33] and "Let him do what he will; he does not sin, if she should marry."[34] The somewhat immoderate departure in demanding the debt from the one or the other sex is given as a concession because of those things which he mentioned before.

(13) Therefore, what he says: "The unmarried woman

____

33. 1 Cor 7.28.   34. 1 Cor 7.36.

thinks about the things of the Lord, that she may be holy in body and spirit,"[35] is not to be understood in such a way that we think a chaste Christian wife is not holy in body. To all the faithful, indeed, it is said: "Do you not know that your bodies are the temple of the Holy Spirit, who is in you, whom you have from God?"[36] Also holy, therefore, are the bodies of married people who remain faithful to themselves and to the Lord.

That an unbelieving spouse does not hinder this sanctity of either of the couple, but, rather, the sanctity of the wife profits the unbelieving husband or the sanctity of the husband profits the unbelieving wife, the same Apostle is a witness when he says: "For the unbelieving husband is sanctified in the wife, and the unbelieving wife is sanctified in the believing husband."[37]

Moreover, this was said in regard to the greater sanctity of the unmarried woman than of the married woman, and a more ample reward is due to this sanctity because it is better than the other good, because she thinks only of this, how she might please the Lord. For it is not that a faithful woman, observing conjugal chastity, does not think how she might please the Lord, but she does so less because she is thinking also of things of the world, how she might please her husband. This is what he wished to say about them, what they can expect, as it were, from the demands of marriage, namely, that they must think of the things of the world, how they might please their husbands.

CHAPTER 14

(17) It is clear that by a subsequent honorable agreement there can be a marriage for those who had not been rightly united.

CHAPTER 15

Once, however, marriage is entered upon in the City [that is, Church] of our God, where also from the first union of the two human beings marriage bears a kind of sacred bond, it can be dissolved in no way except by the death of one of the parties. The bond of marriage remains, even if offspring, for which

---

35. 1 Cor 7.34.   36. 1 Cor 6.19.
37. 1. Cor 7.14.

the marriage was entered upon, should not follow because of a clear case of sterility, so that it is not lawful for married people who know they will not have any children to separate and to unite with others even for the sake of having children. If they do unite, they commit adultery with the ones with whom they join themselves, for they remain married people. It was indeed permissible among the ancients to have another woman with the consent of the wife, from whom common children might be born by the union and seed of the husband, by the privilege and authorization of the wife. Whether this is permissible now, as well, I would not care to say. There is not the need for procreation which there was then, when it was permissible for husbands who could have children to take other women for the sake of a more copious posterity, which certainly is not lawful now. The mysterious difference of times brings so great an opportunity of doing or of not doing something justly that, now, he does better who does not marry even one wife, unless he cannot control himself; then, however, they had without fault several wives, even they who could restrain themselves much more easily, except that piety in that time demanded something else. . . .

CHAPTER 20

(24) Marriage, I say, is a good and can be defended by right reason against all charges. However, with regard to the marriage of the holy patriarchs, I am asking not what marriage but what continence is comparable. Moreover, I am not comparing marriage with marriage—for a gift equal in all things has been given to the mortal nature of man—but men who make use of marriage. Since I do not find any to compare with those men of old who used marriages far differently, it must be asked what continent men can be compared to them—unless, perhaps, Abraham could not restrain himself from marriage because of the kingdom of heaven, who because of the kingdom of heaven could fearlessly immolate his single beloved son on whose account marriage was dear to him.

CHAPTER 22

(27) Accordingly, when even the Law following the time of the patriarchs then called him accursed who did not rear chil-

dren in Israel, even he who could did not show forth this continence, yet he possessed it. Afterwards, the fullness of time came,[38] so that it was said: "Let him accept it who can";[39] from that time up till now and henceforward to the end, he who possesses this continence puts it into practice; he who is unwilling to practice it, let him not say untruthfully that he has it. Therefore, it is with a subtlety that is empty and of no use that they who corrupt good morals by evil conversation[40] say to the Christian man, continent and refusing marriage: "You, then, are better than Abraham?" When he hears this, let him not be troubled or dare to say: "Yes, better," or to fall from his resolution—because the former he does not say truthfully, the latter he does not do rightly—but let him say: "I am indeed not better than Abraham, but the chastity of the unmarried is better than the chastity of marriage. Abraham had one of them in practice, both in habit. He lived chastely in the married state, yet he could have been chaste without marriage, but then it was impossible. I, indeed, more easily do not make use of marriage, which Abraham made use of, than I could make use of marriage as Abraham used it. Therefore, I am better than those who through incontinence of mind cannot do what I am doing. I am not better than those who because of the difference of times did not do what I am doing. What I now do they would have done better, if it was to be done at that time. But what they did I would not be doing as they did, if it had to be done now."

Or, if he feels and knows that he is of such a character that, if he would descend to the use of marriage because of some religious obligation, the virtue of continence remaining safe and secure in the habit of his mind, he would be the type of husband and the type of father that Abraham was, let him openly dare to respond to that captious questioner and to say: "I am not even better than Abraham in at least this type of continence which he did not lack, though it was not apparent; but I am not such a one who has one thing but does another." Let him say these things openly, because, even if he does wish to boast, he will not be foolish, for he speaks the truth. But, if he forbears, lest any man thinks that he is above what he sees

38. Cf. Gal 4.4.   39. Mt 19.12.
40. Cf. 1 Cor 15.33.

in him or hears from him,[41] let him remove from his own person the knot of the question, and let him respond not about the man but about the thing itself, and say: "Who can do so much, he is such a one as Abraham was." Yet, it can happen that the virtue of continence is less in the soul of him who does not make use of marriage which Abraham made use of; still, it is greater than that in the soul of him who on this account observed the chastity of marriage because he could not observe the greater.

The same is the case of the unmarried woman who thinks about the things of the Lord, how she might be holy in body and in spirit.[42] When she hears that impudent inquirer saying: "You are, then, better than Sara?" Let her answer: "I am better, but better than those who lack the virtue of this continence, and I do not believe this in respect to Sara. Therefore, she possessed that virtue and did what was suited to that time. I am free from this duty so that in my body, also, there can appear what she had in her soul."

<h3 style="text-align:center">CHAPTER 23</h3>

(31) In accord with this, that patriarch who was not without a wife was prepared to be without his only son and one to be slain by his own hand.[43] Indeed, I may speak of "his only son" not unfittingly, concerning whom he had heard from the Lord: "Through Isaac shall your descendants be called."[44] Therefore, how much more readily would he have obeyed if it were ordered that he was not to have a wife.

So it is that not in vain do we often wonder at some of both sexes, who, containing themselves from all intercourse, carelessly obey the commands, though they have so ardently embraced the idea of not using things that have been granted. Seeing this, who doubts that the men and women of our times, free from all intercourse but inferior in the virtue of obedi-

---

41. Cf. 2 Cor 12.6.   42. 1 Cor 7.34.

43. Cf. R 2.22: "What I said concerning Abraham . . . I do not entirely approve. It ought to be thought that he believed that his son, if he had been killed, must soon be returned to him by a resurrection from the dead, as it is read in the Epistle to the Hebrews [11.19]."

44. Gn 21.12.

ence, are not rightly compared to the excellence of those holy patriarchs and mothers begetting children, even if the patriarchs had lacked the habit of mind that is manifest in the actions of the men of our day?

Therefore, let the young men singing a new canticle follow the Lamb, as it is written in the Apocalypse: "Who have not defiled themselves with women,"[45] on no other account than that they remained virgins. Let them not think, then, that they are better than the early patriarchs, who used their marriage, if I may put it this way, nuptially. The use, indeed, of marriage is such that there is a defilement if anything is done in marriage through the union of the flesh that exceeds the need for generation, though this is pardonable. For, what does pardon expiate, if that departure does not defile entirely? It would be remarkable if the children following the Lamb were free from this defilement, unless they remained virgins.

CHAPTER 25

(33) Since these things are so, I have answered enough and more than enough to the heretics, whether Manicheans or whoever else calumniate the patriarchs for their many wives, alleging that this is an argument by which they prove their incontinence, if, however, they understand that what is not done contrary to nature is not a sin, since they made use of their wives not for the sake of being wanton, but for procreation; nor against the customs, because at the time those things were being done; nor contrary to the precept, because they were not prohibited by any law. Those, indeed, who illicitly made use of women, either that divine dictum in the Scriptures convicts, or the text puts them before us as ones who are to be judged and avoided, not to be approved or imitated.

CHAPTER 26

(34) However, as much as we can, we advise our people who have spouses not to dare to judge those patriarchs according to their weakness, comparing, as the Apostle says, themselves with themselves,[46] and therefore not understanding what great powers the soul that serves justice has against the passions, so

45. Rv 14.4.   46. Cf. 2 Cor 10.12.

that it does not acquiesce in carnal impulses of this kind and does not allow them to fall into or to proceed to intercourse beyond the need for generation, that is, beyond what the order of nature, beyond what customs, beyond what laws permit.

Men indeed have this suspicion concerning these patriarchs because they themselves either have chosen marriage because of incontinence or they make use of their wives immoderately. But let continent people, either men whose wives have died, or women whose husbands have died, or both, who with equal consent have pledged their continence to God, know that a greater reward is due them than conjugal chastity demands. But, as to the marriage of the holy patriarchs, who were joined in a prophetic way, who neither in intercourse sought anything but progeny, nor anything in the progeny itself except what would profit Christ who was to come in the flesh, let them not only not despise it in comparison with their own resolution, but also in accordance with their own resolution; let them prefer it with hesitation.

(35) Most especially do we warn the young men and the virgins dedicating their virginity to God, so that they may know that they ought to guard the life they are living in the meantime upon earth with the greatest humility, since the greater life which they have vowed is of heaven. For it is written: "The greater you are, the more humble yourself in all things."[47] Therefore, it is for us to say something of their greatness; it is theirs to think of great humility. Thus, with the exception of certain of the married patriarchs and married women of the Old Testament—for these, though they are not married, are not better than they, because if they were married they would not be equal—let them not doubt that all the other married people of this time, even the ones who are continent after experiencing marriage, are surpassed by them, not as much as Susanna is surpassed by Anna, but as much as both are surpassed by Mary. I am speaking of what pertains to the holy integrity of the flesh, for who is ignorant of the other merits that Mary had?

Therefore, let them add a fitting conduct to such a high re-

47. Sir 3.20.

solve, so that they may have a certain security in respect to obtaining such a splendid reward, knowing, indeed, that to themselves and to all the faithful beloved and chosen members of Christ coming from the East and the West, though shining with a light different in each case, because of their merits, this great reward is given in common, to recline with Abraham and Isaac and Jacob in the kingdom of God,[48] who, not for the sake of this world but for the sake of Christ, were spouses, for the sake of Christ were parents.

Augustine continued his mediation of the ascetic debate in his treatise Holy Virginity,[49] *composed just after* The Good of Marriage, *in 401:*

CHAPTER 1

We recently published a book, *The Good of Marriage,*[50] in which we also admonished and warned the virgins of Christ that they must not, because of the superiority of the more perfect gift which they have received from on high, despise, by comparison with themselves, the fathers and mothers[51] of the people of God; and that, because by divine law continence is preferred to matrimony and holy virginity to wedlock, they must not belittle the worth of those men whom the Apostle praises as the olive tree, that the ingrafted wild olive may not boast;[52] who, by the very begetting of children, served the Christ who was to come.

48. Cf. Mt 8.11.
49. FOTC 27.143–147, 154, 160–163, 166–167, 172–173, 177–178.
50. DBC.
51. The patriarchs and holy women of the Old Testament, through whom the Jewish race was propagated.
52. Cf. Rom 11.16–22. St. Paul pictures the Church as an olive tree with its roots anchored deeply in Judaism, thus preserving an organic unity between the Old and the New Dispensations. The full-developed tree is the Church herself. The root and stem are the patriarchs. The many branches are the various members of the Church, some of whom (those of Jewish descent) belong to her by natural growth, while others (the Gentile Christians) have been grafted from wild stock. These latter should preserve a humble respect for the natural branches, and especially for the root and stem; for it is only by being grafted into the stem that the wild branches share in the life of the tree. Cf. S

In them, indeed, were prepared and brought to term those future events which we now behold marvelously and efficaciously fulfilled, of which their conjugal life was, in fact, prophetic.[53] Wherefore, not after the manner of human vows and pleasures, but by the most profound design of God, in some of them fecundity deserved to be honored,[54] in others sterility even merited to become rendered fruitful.[55]

At the present time, however, those to whom it is said: "If they do not have self control, let them marry,"[56] are not to be exhorted, but consoled; but those to whom it is said: "Let him accept it who can,"[57] are to be exhorted lest they be frightened, and to be frightened lest they be proud. Therefore, virginity must not only be praised that it may be loved, but also admonished that it may not be puffed up.

CHAPTER 3

(3) It is written in the Gospel that when the Mother and brethren of Christ, that is, His relatives according to the flesh, were announced to Him, and were waiting outside because they could not get near Him for the crowd, He answered: "Who is my mother, or who are my brethren?" Stretching forth His hand over His disciples, He said: "These are my brethren;

77.10, 201.2, 203.3, and 218.7; also, Fernand Prat, S.J., *The Theology of Saint Paul*, trans. John L. Stoddard (New York: 1927) 2.275–276. St. Augustine here makes particular applications of the analogy in defense of the sacred character of the conjugal life as practiced by the patriarchs.

53. Cf. CF 22.24: "Not only the speech of these men, but their life also was prophetic . . . So, as regards those [Hebrews] who were then made wise of heart in the wisdom of God, . . . a prophecy of the coming of Christ and of the Church ought to be discovered both in what they said and in what they did." It was especially in their conjugal life that they typified the marvelous mysteries that would be revealed in Christ and in His Church. Cf. DBC 16. The patriarchs typified Christ. Their marriage typified His union with the Church. Cf. CF 22.38. Their numerous offspring, constituting the chosen people, typified the multitudes who would be born to the faith through the mystical union of Christ with His Spouse, the Church. Cf. CF 22.57 *et passim*; S 213.7. Even in the practice of polygamy among the patriarchs St. Augustine finds something prophetic; cf. DBC 18.

54. Cf. Gn 12.2, 26.4, and 35.11.

55. Cf. Gn 18.10, 25.21, and 30.22,24.

56. 1 Cor 7.9.   57. Mt 19.12.

and whoever does the will of my Father, he is my brother and mother and sister."[58] What else was He teaching us except to prefer our spiritual kinship to carnal affinity, and that men are not blessed by being connected with just and holy people through blood relationship, but by being united to them through obedience to their teaching and imitation of their life?

Thus, Mary was more blessed in accepting the faith of Christ than in conceiving the flesh of Christ.[59] For, to someone who said: "Blessed is the womb that bore You," He replied: "Rather, blessed are they who hear the word of God and keep it."[60]

Finally, for His brethren, that is, His relatives according to the flesh, who did not believe in Him, of what advantage was that relationship? So, even her maternal relationship would have done Mary no good unless she had borne Christ more happily in her heart than in her flesh.

CHAPTER 4

(4) Indeed, her virginity was itself more beautiful and more pleasing, because Christ, in His conception, did not Himself take away that which He was preserving from violation by man; but, before He was conceived He chose one already consecrated to God of whom He would be born.[61]

The words which Mary addressed to the angel who announced her child to her indicate this. How shall this happen, she asked, "since I do not know man"?[62] And this she would certainly not have said unless she had previously vowed herself to God as a virgin. But, because the customs of the Jews as yet forbade this,[63] she was espoused to a just man; not to one who

58. Mt 12.48–50; also, TEJ 10.3.
59. Cf. TEJ 10.3; CF 29.4; DPMR 2.24; S 69.3, 196.1, 233.3.
60. Lk 11.27–28.
61. Here St. Augustine summarizes the belief in the perpetual virginity of Mary. With St. Ambrose he champions the Catholic doctrine that she was a virgin, not only in the conception of Christ, but also in His birth, and that she remained virginal throughout her life in fulfillment of the vow made to God previous to her marriage. Cf. EAL 34; DBVid 10; CF 29.4; S 69.3, 110.3, 184.1, 191.1, 196.1, 213.7, 215.3, 233.3; *et passim.*
62. Lk 1.34.
63. Perpetual virginity was not unknown among the Jews. The sect of the

would ravage by violence, but to one who would protect against violent men that which she had already vowed.

Although, even if she had only said: "How shall this happen?" and had not added "since I do not know man," she would never have asked at all how a woman was to bear the son promised to her if she had married with the intention of cohabiting.

Again, she could have been commanded to remain a virgin in whom the Son of God would, by a fitting miracle, take upon Himself the nature of a slave,[64] but, in order to be a model for holy virgins, lest it be thought that only she ought to be a virgin who had merited to conceive a child even without carnal intercourse, she consecrated her virginity to God while she was still ignorant of what she would conceive, so that the imitation of the heavenly life in her earthly and mortal body might come about by vow, not by precept, by a love of her own choice, not by the compulsion of obedience.

Thus, Christ, in being born of a virgin who, before she knew who was to be born of her, had resolved to remain a virgin, chose rather to approve holy virginity than to impose it. So, even in that woman in whom He took upon Himself the nature of a slave, He desired virginity to be free.

(12) Let spouses have their blessing, not because they beget children, but because they beget them honorably and lawfully and chastely and for society, and bring up their offspring rightly, wholesomely, and with perseverance; because they keep conjugal fidelity with each other; because they do not desecrate the sacrament[65] of matrimony.

CHAPTER 18

(18) Wherefore, I admonish the men and women who have embraced perpetual continence and sacred virginity to prefer their blessing to marriage in such a way that they may not con-

Essenes demanded absolute continence of its members. However, since the great glory of the race lay in the propagation of the people of God and in providing the carnal generation of the Messiah, marriage and parenthood were more highly esteemed than virginity. Cf. DSV 1.9; DBC 19; DBVid 7.

64. Cf. Phil 2.7.

65. St. Augustine sometimes uses the term "sacrament" in a wide sense for any sacred symbol. Here, however, he employs the term in the strict sense, as it later came to be used exclusively for the seven sacraments.

sider marriage an evil, and may acknowledge that it was not said falsely, but in all truth, by the Apostle: "He who gives his virgin in marriage does well, and he who does not give her does better.[66] . . . And if you take a wife, you have not sinned. And if a virgin marries, she has not sinned"; and a little further on: "But she will be more blessed, in my judgment, if she remains as she is." And, lest it should be regarded as a human judgment, he adds: "And I think that I also have the spirit of God."[67]

This is the teaching of the Lord, the teaching of the Apostle, the true teaching, the sound teaching: so to choose the greater gifts as not to condemn the lesser. The truth of God in the Scripture of God is better than virginity in the mind or in the flesh of any man.

Let what is chaste be so loved that what is true be not denied. For, what evil are they not capable of thinking, even concerning their own flesh, who believe that the tongue of the Apostle, in the very place where it was commending virginity of the body, was itself defiled by the corruption of falsehood?

In the first place, therefore, and above all, let those who choose the blessing of virginity believe with the utmost steadfastness that the holy Scriptures contain no falsehood, and that, therefore, this saying is also true: "And if you take a wife you have not sinned. And if a virgin marries, she has not sinned." And let them not think that so great a blessing of integrity is diminished if marriage shall not be evil. Nay, more, let her rather be confident that a palm of greater glory has been prepared for her who did not fear to be condemned if she married, but who aspired to be more honorably crowned for not marrying.

Wherefore, let not those who have chosen to remain unmarried flee marriage as a pitfall of sin, but let them surmount it as a hill of inferior blessing, that they may come to rest on the mountain of the greater blessing of continence.

Indeed, that hill is dwelt upon under this law, that one may not leave it at will. For "a woman is bound as long as her husband is alive." Truly by it, as by a step, the chastity of widow-

66. 1 Cor 7.38.   67. 1 Cor 7.28 and 40.

hood is reached. But for the sake of virginal chastity, it is either to be avoided by rejecting suitors, or to be surmounted by forestalling suitors.

CHAPTER 19

(19) However, lest anyone think that the rewards of the two works, that is, of the good and of the better, shall be equal, we had to refute those who so interpreted the words of the Apostle: "I think, then, that this is good on account of the present distress," as to claim that virginity is useful, not because of the kingdom of heaven, but because of the present life, as though they who had chosen the higher good were going to possess nothing more than the rest in that eternal life.

In the argument, when we came to this saying of that same Apostle: "Yet such will have tribulation of the flesh. But I spare you that," we turned against the other opponents who did not make nuptials equal to perpetual chastity but who condemned them altogether.

For, while either one is an error, either to make nuptials equal to holy virginity or to condemn them, these two errors, in their overeagerness to avoid each other, attack from opposite extremes, since they have refused to cling to the middle position of truth, in which, both from certain reason and from the authority of the holy Scriptures, we find that marriage is not sinful, yet we do not make it equal to the blessing, either of virginal, or even of widowed continence.

CHAPTER 20

Some, indeed, in embracing virginity, have regarded marriage as a loathsome adultery; others, on the contrary, in defending marriage, have desired the perfection of perpetual continence to merit nothing more than conjugal chastity; as though either the blessing of Susanna[68] were an humiliation of Mary, or Mary's greater blessing ought to be a condemnation of Susanna.

CHAPTER 22

(22) We hope now to demonstrate even more clearly from the most obvious pronouncements of the divine Scriptures

68. Cf. Dn 13. Susanna is a symbol of marital fidelity.

which, within the limits of our memory, we are able to recall, that perpetual continence is to be embraced, not for the sake of the present earthly life, but for the sake of the future life which is promised in the kingdom of heaven.

Who does not, in fact, detect this in the words of the same Apostle, spoken a little later: "He who is unmarried is concerned about the things of the Lord, how he may please the Lord. Whereas he who is married is concerned about the things of the world, how he may please his wife. And the unmarried woman, or the virgin, is set apart. She who is unmarried thinks about the things of the Lord, that she may be holy in body and in spirit. Whereas she who is married thinks about the things of the world, how she may please her husband"?[69]

He certainly does not say: "She is concerned with the things that make for security in this world, that she may pass her time free from more pressing cares." He does not say that the virgin or the unmarried woman is set apart, that is, separated and distinguished from the married woman, for this purpose, that the unmarried woman may be secure in this by avoiding the temporal cares which the wife does not escape; but "she thinks," he says, "about the things of the Lord, how she may please the Lord," and "she thinks about the things of the Lord, that she may be holy in body and in spirit."

Unless, perchance, anyone is even so stupidly contentious that he will attempt to maintain that we desire to please the Lord, not because of the kingdom of heaven, but because of the present world; or that we desire to be holy in body and in spirit for the sake of this life, not for the sake of eternal life.

What is the one who believes this but the most pitiable of all men? For so the Apostle says: "If with this life only in view we have had hope in Christ, we are of all men the most pitied."[70] Is he, indeed, foolish who shares his bread with the hungry, if he does it merely for the sake of this life, and shall he be wise who restrains his body to the extent of continence, by which he refrains even from marriage, if it shall bring him no reward in the kingdom of heaven?

69. Cf. 1 Cor 7.32–34.
70. 1 Cor 15.19.

CHAPTER 26

(26) "What, then," they ask, "does that *denarius*[71] signify, which at the completion of the work in the vineyard is paid equally to all, whether to those who have worked from the first hour, or to those who have worked for one hour?" What, indeed, unless it signifies something which all shall have in common, such as eternal life itself, the very kingdom of heaven, where all shall dwell whom God has predestined, called, justified, and glorified?[72]

"For this corruptible body must put on incorruption, and this mortal body must put on immortality."[73] This is that *denarius*, the reward of all. Nevertheless, "star differs from star in glory. So also with the resurrection of the dead."[74] These are the different rewards of the saints. For, if heaven be signified by that *denarius*, is not to be in heaven common to all the stars? Yet, "there is one glory of the sun, and another glory of the moon, and another of the stars."[75] If the *denarius* were to represent health of body, is not health common to all the members when we are in good health? And if it persist even till death, is it not just as equally present in all? Nevertheless, "God has set the members, each of them, in the body as He willed,"[76] so that it is not all eye, nor all ear, nor all nose; everything else has its own individuality, although it has health in common with all the members.

Thus, because eternal life itself shall belong to all the saints, the same sum of a *denarius* is given to all, but, because in that eternal life the splendor of merits will present a varied luster, "there are many mansions"[77] with the Father. Therefore, in the equality of the *denarius*, one will not live longer than another, but, in the many mansions, one will be honored with greater glory than another.

71. Cf. Mt 20.9–10.
72. Rom 8.30.
73. 1 Cor 15.53.
74. 1 Cor 15.41–42.
75. 1 Cor 15.41.
76. 1 Cor 18.18.
77. Jn 14.2.

CHAPTER 30

(30) You, also, who have not yet vowed this, accept it, you who can.[78] Run with perseverance, "that you may obtain."[79] "Bring up your sacrifices," each one of you, "and come into the courts of the Lord,"[80] not through compulsion, since you are masters of your will. For, not in the same way as it is said: "You shall not commit adultery; you shall not kill,"[81] can it be said: "You shall not marry." Those things are demanded; these are freely offered. If the latter are observed, they merit praise; unless the former are observed, they merit condemnation. In the former, the Lord lays an obligation on you; in the latter, whatever extra you have expended in fulfilling them, He, on His return, will repay you.[82]

Consider the place of honor within His walls (whatever it is) much better than that of sons and daughters; consider there the eternal name.[83] Who will explain what kind of a name it will be? Nevertheless, whatever it will be, it will be eternal. In believing in, and hoping for, and loving this, you have been able, not to avoid a forbidden marriage, but to ascend above a lawful marriage.

Augustine feared that the harmony of the Christian community might be shattered if sexual abstinence were to become the one criterion separating exemplary Christians from more "ordinary" ones. In his Tractates on the Gospel of John, *composed between 407 and 417, he illustrates this point:[84]*

TRACTATE 4.13(2)

(2) Pay attention, my beloved people. There might be in the church some catechumens of more eminent grace. For it sometimes happens that one sees a catechumen who abstains from all sexual intercourse, who renounces the world, who gives up everything he possessed, distributing it to the poor, and he is a catechumen, even instructed, perhaps, in saving doctrine be-

---

78. Mt 19.12.
80. Ps 95(96).8.
82. Cf. Lk 10.35.
84. FOTC 78.103–104.

79. Cf. 1 Cor 9.24.
81. Ex 20.13–14.
83. Is 56.5.

yond many of the faithful. For this man one must feel apprehensive lest he say to himself about holy Baptism by which sins are forgiven, "What more am I going to receive? Look, I am better than this one of the faithful and than that one of the faithful" as he ponders the fact that some of the faithful are married, or perhaps uninstructed, or hold and own their property, while he has already distributed his to the poor. [And this man,] reflecting that he is better than that one who has already been baptized, may disdain to come to Baptism, saying, "Am I to receive this which this man and that man have?" And he may in his own mind review those whom he despises and it may seem to him of virtually no value to receive what lesser men have received, because he already seems to himself to be a better man. And yet all of his sins remain with him; and unless he comes to saving Baptism, where sins are loosed, for all his excellence he cannot enter into the kingdom of heaven.

4

AUGUSTINE'S MATURE POSITION IN
THE ANTI-PELAGIAN WRITINGS

For most of the last two decades of his life, Augustine engaged in debate with various followers of Pelagius. Pelagius, alarmed at the laxity of Christians who excused their sinful behavior on the grounds of their "weakness" and the fatalistic consequences being drawn from the notion of an inherited sin, staunchly upheld the freedom of the human will to choose good as well as evil. According to Pelagius, God has created our natures as good, with the mental and dispositional capacities enabling us to lead righteous lives; He had also instructed us in His laws and given us examples of holy people (including Jesus) in Scripture, and to these aids were added the cleansing power of Baptism that recreates us as "new people." Against Pelagius and his followers, Augustine increasingly emphasized the will's bondage to sin that has been the human condition since the first trespass in Eden. According to Augustine, the guilt of that sin was transmitted to all fetuses through the mechanism of the sinful lust that now spurs and accompanies sexual intercourse—whether those sex acts are performed inside or outside of marriage, whether procreation is intended or not. All children born since the time of Adam and Eve come into the world doomed to death, unable to choose the good without special assistance from God, and with sexual desires that do not obey the governance of the mind and will. Thus the interpretation of Genesis 1–3 was of special importance for Augustine in his explication of how Original Sin came to infect the human race.

In Book 14 of the City of God, *composed around 418–420, Augustine posits that, if Adam and Eve had not sinned in Eden, they would have engaged in sexual intercourse for the procreation of children while enjoying the blessings of Paradise; in this, he sets himself against the teachings of other, more ascetically-minded Church Fathers who did not envision that sexual relations could ever have taken place in a sinless Eden. In the following passages from the* City of God *14, Augustine explains why the sexual act would have been deemed good if the first couple had not sinned, and speculates on how it would have been performed.[1]*

CHAPTER 10

It is quite a different question, and one that deserves attention, whether, even before there was any sin, the first man, or rather our first parents—since there was a marriage of two—experienced any of those passions in their animal body from which we shall be free in our spiritual bodies, once all sin has been purged and brought to an end. If they did, how could they have been perfectly happy in that marvelous place called Paradise? How, in fact, can anyone be called absolutely happy if he suffers from fear or sorrow? On the other hand, what could have made our first parents either fearful or sorrowful, surrounded as they were by an abundance of good things, in a place where there was neither death nor ill health to be feared, where nothing was lacking that a well-ordered will could long for, and where nothing was present that could hinder man's material or mental happiness?

The love of our first parents for God was perfectly serene and their mutual affection was that of a true and faithful married couple. And their love brought them immense joy since the object of their love was always theirs to enjoy. There was a calm turning away from sin which, so long as it lasted, kept evil of every other kind from saddening their lives. . . .

Now, this happiness of our first parents, undisturbed by any passion and undiminished by any pain, is the measure of the happiness which the entire human race would have enjoyed if Adam and Eve had not been guilty of the evil which they have transmitted to posterity or if no one of their descendants had

1. FOTC 14.373–375, 377–379, 388–389, 395–396, 402–403, 405–407.

committed any wickedness worthy of damnation. And this happiness would have continued until, in virtue of God's blessing, "Be fruitful and multiply,"[2] the number of the elect had been completed; after which, another even more perfect happiness was to be given, like that which the blessed angels enjoy, a happiness which would have excluded even the possibility of sin or of death, so that the saints would have lived on earth just as exempt from all labor, pain, and death as will now be their lot to live only after all such things have been suffered and they shall be clothed with incorruptible bodies in the final resurrection.

Augustine depicts the serpent's approach to Eve that initiated sin:

CHAPTER 11

This Lucifer, striving to insinuate his sly seductions into the minds of man whose fidelity he envied, since he himself had fallen, chose for his spokesman a serpent in the terrestrial Paradise, where all the animals of earth were living in harmless subjection to Adam and Eve. It was suited for the task because it was a slimy and slippery beast that could slither and twist on its tortuous way. So, subjecting it to his diabolical design by the powerful presence of his angelic nature and misusing it as his instrument, he, at first, parleyed cunningly with the woman as with the weaker part of that human society, hoping gradually to gain the whole. He assumed that a man is less gullible and can be more easily tricked into following a bad example than into making a mistake himself. This was the case with Aaron. He did not consent to the making of idols for his erring people, but he gave an unwilling assent when he was asked by the people to do so;[3] and it is not to be thought that Solomon was deceived into believing in the worship of idols, but was merely won over to this sacrilege by feminine flattery.[4] So, too, we must believe that Adam transgressed the law of God, not because he was deceived into believing that the lie was true, but because in obedience to a social compulsion he yielded to Eve, as hus-

---

2. Gn 1.28.   3. Ex 32.2 and 21–24.
4. 1 Kgs 11.4.

band to wife, as the only man in the world to the only woman. It was not without reason that the Apostle wrote, "Adam was not deceived but the woman was deceived."[5] He means, no doubt, that Eve accepted the serpent's word as true, whereas Adam refused to be separated from his partner even in a union of sin—not, of course, that he was, on that account, any less guilty, since he sinned knowingly and deliberately. That is why the Apostle does not say: "He did not sin," but "he was not deceived." Elsewhere, he implies that Adam did sin: "Through one man sin entered into the world." And a little further on, even more plainly, he adds: "After the likeness of the transgression of Adam."[6] The distinction is here made between those who, like Adam, sin with full knowledge and those who are deceived because they do not know that what they are doing is a sin. It is this distinction which gives meaning to the statement: "Adam was not deceived."

Nevertheless, in so far as he had had no experience of the divine severity, Adam could be deceived in believing that his transgression was merely venial. And, therefore, he was at least not deceived in the same way that Eve was; he was merely mistaken concerning the judgment that would follow his attempt to excuse himself: "The woman you placed at my side gave me fruit from the tree and I ate."[7]

To summarize briefly: though not equally deceived by believing the serpent, they equally sinned and were caught and ensnared by the Devil.

According to Augustine, the first sin changed human nature forever. One result of the sin was our inability to control our sexual organs, as manifested both in raging lust and in unhappy impotence:

CHAPTER 16

There are, then, many kinds of lusts for this or that, but when the word is used by itself without specification it suggests to most people the lust for sexual excitement. Such lust does not merely invade the whole body and outward members; it

5. 1 Tm 2.14.   6. Rom 5.12 and 14.
7. Gn 2.12.

takes such complete and passionate possession of the whole man, both physically and emotionally, that what results is the keenest of all pleasures on the level of sensation; and, at the crisis of excitement, it practically paralyzes all power of deliberate thought.

This is so true that it creates a problem for every lover of wisdom and holy joys who is both committed to a married life and also conscious of the apostolic ideal, that every one should "learn how to possess his vessel in holiness and honor, not in the passion of lust like the Gentiles who do not know God."[8] Any such person would prefer, if this were possible, to beget his children without suffering this passion. He could wish that, just as all his other members obey his reason in the performance of their appointed tasks, so the organs of parenthood, too, might function in obedience to the orders of will and not be excited by the ardors of lust.

Curiously enough, not even those who love this pleasure most—whether legitimately or illegitimately indulged—can control their own indulgences. Sometimes, their lust is most importunate when they least desire it; at other times, the feelings fail them when they crave them most, their bodies remaining frigid when lust is blazing in their souls. And so, strangely, lust serves neither the will to generate, nor lust for its own source; and the very passion that so often joins forces to resist the soul is sometimes so divided against itself that, after it has roused the soul to passion, it refuses to awaken the feelings of the flesh.

Thus, feelings of shame about our sexual organs, as well as the desire for privacy at the moment of marital intercourse, testify to the presence of Original Sin's effects even among baptized Christians. Augustine imagines that the sexual relation of Adam and Eve in Eden, had they remained sinless, would have been quite different:

CHAPTER 21

No one, then, should dream of believing that the kind of lust which made the married couple in the Garden ashamed

---

8. 1 Thes 4.4.

of their nakedness was meant to be the only means of fulfilling
the command which God gave when He "blessed them, saying:
'Increase and multiply, and fill the earth.'"[9] The fact is that
this passion had no place before they sinned; it was only after
the fall, when their nature had lost its power to exact obedience
from the sexual organs, that they fell and noticed the loss and,
being ashamed of their lust, covered these unruly members.
But God's blessings on their marriage, with the command to
increase and multiply and fill the earth, was given before the
fall. The blessing remained even when they had sinned, because it was a token that the begetting of children is a part of
the glory of marriage and has nothing to do with the penalty
for sin.

Rejecting an allegorical interpretation of the words "male" and "fe-
male" as used in the creation story, Augustine explains how he imagines
the physical act of sexual intercourse would have occurred in Eden if
Adam and Eve had not sinned:

CHAPTER 24

In Paradise, then, generative seed would have been sown by
the husband and the wife would have conceived as need required, and all would have been achieved by deliberate choice
and not by uncontrollable lust. After all, it is not only our hands
and fingers, feet and toes, made up of joints and bones that we
move at will, but we can also control the flexing and stiffening
of muscles and nerves, as when we voluntarily wrinkle our face
or pout with our lips. So, too, with the lungs, which are the
most delicate of human organs next to the brain, and need the
protection of a wall of ribs. Whether we inhale or exhale or
make or modify sounds as in puffing, panting, talking, shout-
ing and singing, the lungs obey our will as readily as the bellows
obey a blacksmith or an organist. It is worth mentioning in
passing that some of the animals can move their skin in a particular spot where something is felt that ought to be removed
as when they shake off a fly or, in some cases, even expel a spear
from where it is lodged. Merely because men have no such

9. Gn 1.28.

power is no reason why God could not give it to any animals He wanted to. Nor is there any reason why man should not have had control even over those lowly organs which have been so rebellious ever since man's own rebellion against God. As far as God is concerned, there was no difficulty in making men in such a way that organs which are now excited only by lust could have been completely controlled by deliberate choice. . . .

CHAPTER 26

Now, the point about Eden was that a man could live there as a man longs to live, but only so long as he longed to live as God willed him to live. Man in Eden lived in the enjoyment of God and he was good by a communication of the goodness of God. His life was free from want, and he was free to prolong his life as long as he chose. There were food and drink to keep away hunger and thirst and the tree of life to stave off death from senescence. There was not a sign or a seed of decay in man's body that could be a source of any physical pain. Not a sickness assailed him from within, and he feared no harm from without. His body was perfectly healthy and his soul completely at peace. And as in Eden itself there was never a day too hot or too cold, so in Adam, who lived there, no fear or desire was ever so passionate as to worry his will. Of sorrows there was none at all and of joys none that was vain, although a perpetual joy that was genuine flowed from the presence of God, because God was loved with a "charity from a pure heart and a good conscience and faith unfeigned."[10] Family affection was ensured by purity of love; body and mind worked in perfect accord; and there was an effortless observance of the law of God. Finally, neither leisure nor labor had ever to suffer from boredom or sloth.

How in the world, then, can any one believe that, in a life so happy and with men so blessed, parenthood was impossible without the passion of lust? Surely, every member of the body was equally submissive to the mind and, surely, a man and his wife could play their active and passive roles in the drama of conception without the lecherous promptings of lust, with perfect serenity of soul and with no sense of disintegration be-

10. 1 Tm 1.5.

tween body and soul. Merely because we have no present experience to prove it, we have no right to reject the possibility that, at a time when there was no unruly lust to excite the organs of generation and when all that was needed was done by deliberate choice, the seminal flow could have reached the womb with as little rupture of the hymen and by the same vaginal ducts as is at present the case, in reverse, with the menstrual flux. And just as the maturity of the fetus could have brought the child to birth without the moanings of the mother in pain, so could connection and conception have occurred by a mutually deliberate union unhurried by the hunger of lust.

Perhaps these matters are somewhat too delicate for further discussion. It must suffice to have done the best that I could to suggest what was possible in the Garden of Eden, before there was any need for the reins of reticence to bridle a discussion like this. However, as things now are, the demands of delicacy are more imperative than those of discussion. The trouble with the hypothesis of a passionless procreation controlled by will, as I am here suggesting it, is that it has never been verified in experience, not even in the experience of those who could have proved that it was possible. Actually, they sinned too soon and brought on themselves exile from Eden. Hence, today it is practically impossible even to discuss the hypothesis of voluntary control without the imagination being filled with the realities of rebellious lust. It is this last fact which explains my reticence; not, certainly, any lack of proof for the conclusion my mind has reached.

Augustine's interest in promoting a moderate form of asceticism also extended to the period of his anti-Pelagian writings. In 414, for example, he wrote a treatise for a wealthy and aristocratic widow, Juliana, counseling her not to remarry. A position that he had developed in arguing against Manichean detractors of Scripture, namely, that the "difference of times" allowed for the variation in sexual and marital standards appropriate to the Old Testament heroes and to Christians in the present era, is here again rehearsed. Most importantly, Augustine's past concerns intersect in this treatise with his more recent need to refute Pelagian teaching. Since Juliana and her family enjoyed a friendly relationship with Pelagius,[11] Augustine wished to warn her, albeit discreetly, not to accept Pelagius' views concerning the self-sufficiency of the human will for the accomplishment of virtuous behavior. Thus he reminds Juliana that the ability to lead a chaste life is always a gift of God, not the result of human effort alone. Augustine's advice to Juliana is contained in his treatise, The Excellence of Widowhood. *Some passages from that work are included here:[12]*

CHAPTER 4

You see from the foregoing that conjugal chastity and fidelity to the bond of Christian marriage is a gift, and that this gift is from God, so that if the concupiscence of the flesh in wedlock exceeds to some extent the measure required for the procreation of children, this is not an evil of the married state, but is venial because of the good of marriage.[13] When the Apostle declares: "But this I say by way of concession, not by way of commandment," he is not referring to the union contracted for the procreation of children, nor to the faith of conjugal chastity, nor to the sacrament of matrimony, indissoluble as long as both partners live, all of which are good, but to that inordinate gratification of the senses among married persons, which is due to their infirmity and which is condoned by the intervention of the good proper to marriage. Likewise, when he says: "A woman is bound as long as her husband is alive, but if her husband dies, she is free. Let her marry whom she pleases, only let it be in the Lord. But she will be more blessed, in my judgment, if she remains as she is,"[14] he clearly shows that, even when a Christian woman marries again after the death of her husband, she is blessed in the Lord, but that a widow is more blessed in the same Lord; that is to say, if I may

11. For the connections, see Peter Brown, "Pelagius and His Supporters: Aims and Environment," *Journal of Theological Studies* N.S. 19 (1968) 93–114, and "The Patrons of Pelagius: The Roman Aristocracy between East and West," *Journal of Theological Studies* N.S. 21 (1970) 56–72, both reprinted in Brown's *Religion and Society in the Age of Saint Augustine* (1972).

12. FOTC 16.283, 288–292, 302–307.

13. Though St. Augustine lamented the evils arising from the relation of the concupiscence of the flesh to marriage, he was always firm in his defense of matrimony and its threefold goods.

14. 1 Cor 7.39–40.

make use of the examples as well as the words of the Scriptures, Ruth was blessed, but Anna was more blessed.[15]

The role of holy women was different in the times of the Prophets. Obedience, not concupiscence, impelled women to marry for the propagation of the People of God, among whom the forerunners of Christ were sent in advance. For, this People, by the things that happened to them as a type,[16] whether they recognized these types or not, were indeed the prophet of Christ, from whom Christ was to take flesh. Hence, in order that this race might be multiplied, the man who did not raise up seed in Israel was held accursed by sentence of the law.[17] That is why holy women were animated by the pious desire of offspring rather than by concupiscence; we may rightly believe that they would not have sought the marriage union if issue could have been obtained in any other way. Men were permitted to have several living wives. That provision for the propagation of the race, and not concupiscence of the flesh, was the reason for this custom is evident from the fact that, though holy men might have several wives, holy women were not allowed to be united with several husbands at the same time, for it was considered shameful for them to seek unions that would not render them more fruitful. When the pious Ruth did not have offspring at the death of her husband, as was required in Israel at that time, she sought another union in order to fulfill this requirement. More blessed than this twice-married woman, however, was Anna, the widow of one husband, because she merited the privilege of being a prophetess of Christ. She may or may not have had children—the silence of Scripture leaves this point in doubt—yet we may believe that the same Spirit which enabled her to recognize the Holy Infant also enabled her to foresee that Christ was soon to be born of a virgin. Even though childless—that is, if she had no children—she was justified in renouncing a second marriage because she realized that the time had come when Christ might be served more perfectly, not by the office of motherhood, but by the practice of

15. Cf. Lk 2.36–38.   16. Cf. 1 Cor 10.11.
17. Cf. Dt 25.5–10.

continence; not by the fruitfulness of marriage, but by the chaste conduct of widowhood. But, if Ruth was conscious of the propagation in her flesh of that seed from which Christ would take flesh, and in marrying was motivated by this knowledge, I no longer have the presumption to say that the widowhood of Anna was more blessed than the fecundity of Ruth.

CHAPTER 8

(11) As for you, you both have children and live in that end of the world when the time has already come not "to scatter stones, but to gather; not to embrace but to refrain from embraces"[18]—when the Apostle cries out: "But this I say, brethren, the time is short; it remains that those who have wives be as if they had none."[19] Surely, if you had sought a second marriage, it would not have been in obedience to a prophecy or a law, or even the desire of the flesh for offspring, but merely a sign of incontinence. You would have followed the advice of the Apostle, when, after having said: "It is good for them if they so remain, even as I," he immediately added: "But if they do not have self-control, let them marry, for I prefer them to marry rather than to burn."[20] He said this for the benefit of those whom the evil of unbridled lust might lead into criminal indulgence if it were not restrained by honorable marriage. But, thanks to the Lord, you have brought into the world what you did not wish to be, and the virginity of your daughter has compensated for the loss of your own virginity. A careful inquiry into Christian doctrine reveals that in these our times first marriages should be rejected if incontinence is not an impediment. For, he who said: "If they do not have self-control, let them marry," could have said: "If they do not have children, let them marry," if now, after the resurrection and the promulgation of the teachings of Christ, when there is such a multitude of children in all nations to be born of the spirit, the duty of bringing forth children in the flesh were such as it was in former times. When the Apostle says elsewhere: "I desire therefore that the younger widows marry, bear children, rule

18. Cf. Eccl 3.5. 19. 1 Cor 7.29.
20. Cf. 1 Cor 7.8–9.

their households,"[21] he recommends the good of marriage with wisdom and apostolic authority; he does not impose the duty of bearing children, as a law to be observed, upon those who have chosen the state of continence. Finally, he makes it clear why he has said this, by adding: "Give the adversary no occasion for abusing us. For already some have turned aside after Satan."[22] By these words he wishes us to understand that, for the young widows whom he desired to marry, continence would have been better than marriage, but that it was better for them to marry than to turn aside after Satan, that is, by looking back to former things after having chosen the excellent state of chastity in virginity or widowhood, to abandon it and to perish. Accordingly, let those who do not have self-control marry rather than embrace the profession of continence, rather than pledge themselves by vow to God, for, if they do not keep their promise made to God, they will be deserving of just condemnation. Concerning such persons, he says in another place: "For when they have wantonly turned away from Christ, they wish to marry, and are to be condemned, because they have broken their first troth,"[23] that is, they have abandoned the state of continence for the sake of marriage. They have indeed broken their troth, because they have not persevered in the observance of the vow to which they had previously pledged themselves. The good of marriage is always a good, but in former times among the People of God it was an act of obedience to law; now, it is a remedy for infirmity and for some a solace for their human nature. The desire to have offspring, not through promiscuous unions as among animals, but within the bonds of honorable marriage, is a human instinct that is deserving of no blame. Nevertheless, the Christian soul, intent upon heavenly things, attains greater merit by rising above this inclination and keeping it in subjection.

CHAPTER 16

(20) In the introduction I indicated the two main divisions of this small treatise and I promised that the first part would be devoted to instruction and the second to exhortation. This

21. 1 Tm 5.14.   22. 1 Tm 5.15.
23. 1 Tm. 5.11–12.

first part I have now completed to the best of my ability, considering the difficulty of the subject. Let us now go on to the exhortation in order that you may take delight in the fervent practice of that good which you now have the wisdom to understand. In the first place, I exhort you to attribute any predilection you may have for holy chastity to the grace of God, and to return thanks to Him, who by His Spirit has so bountifully poured forth His charity in your heart[24] that for the love of a higher good you have renounced the right of a lawful union. He has given you the grace not to desire marriage, although it was lawful, and, by rendering it unlawful even if you should desire it, has made your determination to renounce it more steadfast, lest you should do now, when it is forbidden, what you did not do when it was permitted. As a widow consecrated to Christ, you have merited the privilege of seeing your daughter a virgin consecrated to Christ. While you pray after the example of Anna, she follows the example of Mary. The more you recognize these favors to be the gifts of God, the more blessed you will be in these same gifts; in fact, you are not blessed unless you know from whom you have what you have. Consider what the Apostle says on this point: "Now we have received not the spirit of the world, but the spirit that is from God, that we may know the things that have been given us by God."[25] Many, indeed, have manifold gifts from God, and, not knowing from whom they have received them, they boast of them with impious vanity. No one, however, is blessed by the gifts of God unless he is grateful to the Giver. It is only by the grace of Him who commands us that we are able to obey the admonition, "Lift up your hearts," in the sacred mysteries;[26] and then, in order that we may not attribute the glory to ourselves for the great grace of having our hearts lifted up as though it were in our own power, these words follow: "Let us

24. Cf. Rom 5.5.   25. Cf. 1 Cor 2.12.

26. The Eucharastic Sacrifice. In this passage, St. Augustine quotes from the dialogue that introduces the Preface of the Mass. This prayer and the Canon date from the earliest ages of the Church. The dialogue is first found in the *Apostolica Traditio* of Hippolytus, written about 218. Cf. De Puniet, *La liturgie de la Messe*, Ch. 5; also Cyprian, *De Oratione Dominica* 31 (PL 4.358); Cyril of Jerusalem, *Catechesis Mystagogica* 5.4–5 (PG 33.1111); and *Constitutiones Apostolicae* 8.12 (PG 1.1091).

give thanks to the Lord our God." And immediately we are reminded of the response: "It is meet, it is just." You recognize the source of these words and you also know by what authority and with what great sacredness they are recommended to us. Hold fast and cherish what you have received and give thanks to the Giver. Although it is in your power to receive and to have, nevertheless you possess that which you have received; for, to a proud person glorying in what he had received as though he had received it from himself, the Truth declares in the words of the Apostle: "What have you that you have not received? And if you have received it, why do you boast as if you had not received it?"[27]

CHAPTER 17

(21) I feel compelled to discuss this question in order to warn you against the insidious discourses of certain persons[28] who must be shunned and avoided. They are beginning to corrupt the minds of their hearers, and it must be said with tears that they are hostile to the grace of Christ, for they would persuade us to regard as unnecessary the prayer to the Lord that we may not enter into temptation. As champions of the free will of man, they try to prove that we can fulfill the divine commandments by our will alone, without the assistance of God's grace. From this teaching it would follow that the Lord spoke to no purpose when He said: "Watch and pray, that you may not enter into temptation,"[29] and that to no purpose we daily say in the Lord's Prayer itself: "Lead us not into temptation."[30] If to overcome temptation is already in our power, why do we pray that we may not enter into it or be brought into it? We should rather do what depends upon our own free will and unrestricted power, and scorn the Apostle when he says: "God is faithful and will not permit you to be tempted beyond your strength,"[31] and we should defy him, saying: "Why do I ask from God what has been placed in my own power?" Far be it from one who is in his right mind to reason in this manner.

27. 1 Cor 4.7.
28. The reference here is to Pelagius.
29. Mt 26.41.   30. Mt 6.13.
31. 1 Cor 10.13.

Therefore, let us beg Him to give us what He commands us to have. He commands us to have what we do not yet possess, in order to remind us of what we should ask. And when we find that we have the power to do what He has commanded, we should understand from whom we have received it, lest, being puffed up and carried away by the spirit of the world, we should be unmindful of the things that have been given us by God.[32] Therefore, we do not destroy the freedom of the human will when we acknowledge with pious gratitude the grace of God by which the will is assisted, and do not reject it with ungrateful self-sufficiency. It is indeed within our power to will, but the will itself is admonished that it may be stirred to action, healed that it may be strong, enlarged that it may receive, and replenished that it may have abundantly. If we did not exercise our will, we certainly would not receive, nor would we possess, those things that are given to us. Who, indeed, would have continence—if, among the other gifts of God, I may single out the one that I am now discussing with you—who, I say, would have continence if he did not will it? No one would receive this virtue unless he willed it. But, if you wish to understand to whom we owe the power of the will to receive and to possess, consult Scripture; or, rather, since you already know this, reflect upon the words you have read: "As I knew that no one could be continent except God gave it, and this also was a point of wisdom, to know whose gift it was."[33] Great are these two gifts, wisdom and continence: wisdom, by which we are formed in the knowledge of God; continence, by which we are no longer conformed to this world. God commands us, however, to be wise and to be continent, for without these virtues[34] it is impossible for us to be just and perfect. Let us pray, then, that He who has prescribed what we ought to will by precept and counsel may by His assistance and inspiration give us what He commands. Let us pray that He preserve what He has given us, and let us entreat Him to supply what He has not yet given; let us pray still and give thanks for the gifts already received and have confidence that we shall obtain those we expect, for the very reason that we are grateful for those we have received. For He who

32. Cf. 1 Cor 2.12.   33. Wis 8.21.
34. For *bonis* several of the less reliable MSS have *donis*.

faithful married persons the grace to refrain
...ion and adultery also gives to holy virgins and
...s the grace to abstain from all carnal intercourse; rightly,
therefore, is the name of chastity or continence given to this
virtue. Granted that we have received continence from Him,
do we, perhaps, have wisdom from ourselves? What, then, do
these words of the Apostle James signify: "If any of you is want-
ing in wisdom, let him ask it of God, who gives abundantly to
all men, and does not reproach; and it will be given to him"?[35]
With the assistance of the Lord I have already treated this question rather extensively in other brief works of mine, and with
His help I shall discuss it further when I have the occasion to
do so.[36]

*Julian of Eclanum, Augustine's last major Pelagian opponent,
pressed home the negative implications of Augustine's position on Original Sin, namely, that Augustine's view of the sexual transmission of
Original Sin implied that marriage was evil.[37] For Julian, sexual desire
was part of created human nature and, when expressed in a lawful
marriage, should be seen as good. To him, Augustine's position sounded
outrightly "Manichean," as if God's creation of two sexes were a mistake, as if reproduction were an evil, as if marriage had been invented
by the devil, as if the sexual act of a married couple were tantamount
to the "murder" of their offspring by its necessary imprinting on them
of the sin that would lead to their damnation. In response to Julian's
critique and taunts, Augustine formulated his fullest statement on
Original Sin, lust, the goodness of marriage and reproduction, and
the justice of God in his damning and saving activities. Augustine
wished to stress that, although fetuses are doomed because of their in-
fection with Original Sin, the saving power of God reached even to
babies: God condemned, but God also saved. Christian parents do not
have the ability to pass on to their children at the time of conception
their own Christian regeneration, but only their old, unredeemed nature; thus God's unmerited grace must come anew to every child who*

35. Jas 1.5.
36. Previous to the date of this work, St. Augustine had written the following anti-Pelagian treatises: DPMR (c.412), DSL (412), and DFO (413).
37. For an overview of Julian's position, see Brown, *The Body and Society*,
pp. 408–415.

is to receive Christian salvation. God has indeed organized the world in a way that is both just and good, Augustine argued. In Against Julian, *dated to 421–422, he sets forth these positions. The "you" whom Augustine addresses is Julian,[38] to whose now-lost book* To Turbantius *he responds.*

BOOK TWO, CHAPTER 1

(3) If you would diligently investigate these things and not oppose with unbelieving boldness those things which are founded on the ancient truth of the Catholic faith, then, nourished by the grace of Christ, you would come to those things which have been hidden from the wise and prudent and revealed to the little ones.[39] For great is the extent of the sweetness of the Lord, which He did not begrudge, yet hid for those who fear Him, and accomplished for those who hope not in themselves but in Him.[40] Therefore we say what that faith holds, of which it is written: "Unless you believe you will not understand."[41] Not the Devil, but the true and truly good God, is the Creator of men, ineffably producing the clean even from the unclean, although no man is born clean; hence, until he is cleansed by the Holy Spirit, he is obliged to be subject to the unclean spirit. And no uncleanness of the natures, however great it be, is any crime of marriage, for the proper good of marriage is plainly distinct from many faults of the natures. And no guilt of sin remains which is not removed by the regeneration which is made in Christ, although a weakness remains, and he who is reborn, if he makes progress, fights against this within himself. Nor is God unjust, since He renders what is due to sins either original or personal;[42] rather would He be shown to be unjust or weak if He Himself, without pre-

---

38. FOTC 35.56–57, 120–121, 145, 152–153, 198–200, 210–211, 282, 285, 287–290, 295, 301, 333, 350–351.

39. Mt 11.25.   40. Ps 30(31).20.

41. Is 7.9 (LXX).

42. In this book the Latin word *originale*—which, for the sake of clarity and adherence to custom, is here translated by the English "Original"—is seldom used with the meaning "first," or "initial," as is often true in ordinary English usage, but is best read as "by way of origin" or "by means of origin." "Origin" itself most often means "origination," signifying the action of arising from a source.

ceding sin either original or personal, put "the heavy yoke upon the children of Adam, from the day of their coming out of their mother's womb until the day of their burial into the mother of all,"[43] as is written, under which yoke His image is defaced, or if someone else put it upon them against His will. Nor is the perfection of virtue to be despaired of through the grace of Him who can change and heal a nature vitiated from its origin.

BOOK THREE, CHAPTER 16

(16) You proceed to construct your second syllogism; I say it is yours, since the first syllogism was also yours, not mine.[44] You say: "The reason for the existence of the sexes is the union of bodies," and you want me to concede this to you. I do concede it. You continue: "If the union of bodies is always evil, the condition of bodies in the different sexes is a deformity." If this argument were good, it would not disturb me, for I do not say that nuptial union—that is, union for the purpose of procreating—is evil, but even say it is good. But it does not follow, if the union of the two sexes is always evil in fact, that the condition of the bodies in the different sexes is a deformity. If men were subject to the evil of lust to such an extent that if the honesty of marriage were removed, all of them would have intercourse indiscriminately, in the manner of dogs, the condition of the bodies, of which God is the author, would not be a deformity merely because all sexual union happened to be evil. Even now, in evil adulterous union, we see that the work of God in the condition of the bodies is good. Yon see how logically you have said nothing, but that is no reflection on the art of dialectics from whose principles you have much departed. You use it to glorify yourself and shock the inexperienced in your desire to appear what you are not. But, even if you were an excellent dialectician, you would be at a loss as to how these matters should be discussed; as matters stand, you are both inept and unskilled. If you were a good dialectician, you would still be an inept artist. Yet you advance to the combat as though

43. Sir 40.1.
44. The second of the syllogisms by Julian is the first part of a *reductio ad absurdum* which is completed by the third syllogism below.

you were laden with the darts of dialectics, and you hurl these laden daggers, saying: "If intercourse is always evil, the condition of bodies in the different sexes is a deformity." When you add that I cannot deny this, you do not see that what you have called a necessary argument is not consequent. What is it that I cannot deny, unthinking man? What am I unable to deny? It is this, which you cannot deny—if you grasp it even so tardily: that, if the intercourse of adulterers is evil, it is not therefore true that the condition of those born of it is a deformity. Evil union is the work of the men operating evilly from their good members. The condition of the newborn is the work of God operating well from evil men. If you say that, even when there is adultery, the union is good in itself, since it is natural, but adulterers use it evilly, why will you not acknowledge that in the same way lust can be evil, yet the married may nevertheless use it well for the purpose of begetting children? Will you assert there can be evil use of good, but there cannot be good use of evil? We see how well the Apostle used Satan himself, when he delivered a man over to him for the destruction of the flesh, that his spirit might be saved in the day of the Lord, and when he delivered others up to him that they might learn not to blaspheme.[45]

BOOK THREE, CHAPTER 21

(43) In what do your "glorious combats" of the holy virgins consist, except that they are not conquered by evil, but conquer the evil in good? I prefer to call these combats more glorious, not merely glorious, for conjugal chastity also has its victory, although lesser, from the subjugation of this evil. It, too, combats carnal concupiscence lest it exceed the proprieties of the marriage bed; it combats lest concupiscence break into the time agreed upon by the spouses for prayer. If this conjugal chastity possesses such great power and is so great a gift from God that it does what the matrimonial code prescribes, it combats in even more valiant fashion in regard to the act of conjugal union, lest there be indulgence beyond what suffices for generating offspring. Such chastity abstains during menstruation and pregnancy, nor has it union with one no longer able to

---

45. Cf. 1 Cor 5.5.

conceive on account of age. And the desire for union does not prevail, but ceases when there is no prospect of generation. But if an act is done in regard to the spouse, not contrary to nature, yet passing beyond the limit of the matrimonial code, then, according to the Apostle,[46] it is something pardonable, because the carnal limit is not exceeded, yet, lest the limit itself be exceeded, there must be warfare against the evil of concupiscence, which is so evil it must be resisted in the combat waged by chastity, lest it do damage.

BOOK THREE, CHAPTER 22

(51) Since these things are so, we see that marriage, as marriage, is good, and man, be he born of marriage or of adultery, is good in so far as he is man, because, in so far as he is a man, he is the work of God; yet, because generated with and from the evil which conjugal chastity uses well, it is necessary that he be freed from the bond of this evil by regeneration. Why do you ask where original sin is, when the lust against which you fight in yourself speaks to you more eloquently than you yourself speak when you praise it? Why do you ask: "Whence does man, whom God made, come to be under the power of the Devil?" Whence does he come under a death which God did not make? You ask: "What does the Devil recognize as his own, if he made neither what was made, nor whence it was made?" What was made is man; whence it is made, the seed of man. Both are good; the Devil made neither, but sowed the fault of the seed. The Devil does not recognize there his own good, because the good we both praise is not his; but he recognizes his own evil, against which we both fight, and it is not right that what we both fight against is praised by one of us. Surely you realize that when you ask me: "Among so many goods, whence comes the evil in infants?" you pass by what I wrote in the same book you are answering; among the statements you are now answering I quote the Apostle's words: "Through one man sin entered into the world, and through sin death, and thus passed unto all men; in whom all have sinned."[47] You do not want anyone to hear or to read this in that passage where it is most nec-

46. Cf. 1 Cor 7.6.
47. Rom 5.12.

essary, lest they recognize their own faith, and despise your arguments.

(34) I did not write the words you quote from me, saying: "The reason children are under the power of the Devil is that they are born of the union of bodies." To say "who are born of the union of the bodies" is not the same as to say "because they are born of the union of the bodies." The cause of the evil here is not their being born of the union of bodies, since, even if human nature had not been vitiated by the sin of the first man, children could not have been generated except from the union of bodies. The reason those born of the union of bodies are under the power of the Devil before they are reborn through the Spirit is that they are born through that concupiscence by which the flesh lusts against the spirit and forces the spirit to lust against the flesh.[48] There would be no such combat between good and evil if no one had sinned. Just as there was no combat before man's iniquity, so there will be no combat after man's infirmity.

(35) You argue against my words at length: "Because we are made up of elements of unequal goodness, the soul ought to rule over the body. The one we have in common with the gods; the other, with the beasts. Therefore, that which is better, the soul endowed with virtue, should rule both the members of the body and its desires." You fail to observe that desires are not ruled as members are. Desires are evils which we restrain by reason and fight against with our mind; members are goods which we move by the decision of the will, with the exception of the reproductive members, although they also are the work of God and are good. They are called *pudenda* because lust has greater power to move them than reason, although we do not permit them to commit the acts to which they urge us, since we can easily control the other members. But, when does a man use his good members badly except when he consents to the evil desires within him? Of these desires, lust is baser than oth-

48. Gal 5.17.

ers, and if not resisted it commits horrible impurities. Conjugal modesty alone uses this evil well. This lust is not an evil in beasts, because in them it does not war against reason, which they lack. Why do you not believe that it could have been divinely granted to those in Paradise before there was sin that they might without any lust procreate children by tranquil action and the union or intercourse of the members of the body; or, at least, that lust in them was such that its action neither preceded nor exceeded the will? Or do you count it nothing to approve of lust unless it be approved as that which solicits the unwilling and even those who fight against it? This is the kind of lust over which the Pelagians glory, even in its strife, as though over a good. But the saints confess it with groaning, that they may be delivered from evil.

BOOK FOUR, CHAPTER 8

(49) Who says: "Evil exists in the conjugal members," when marriage uses well the evil of concupiscence for the purpose of propagating children? This concupiscence would not be an evil if it were moved only to lawful union for the sole purpose of generating; but, as it is, conjugal modesty, resisting it, becomes the limit of evil and is therefore a good. Your slander, that "Its crime goes unpunished because of religion," is false because no crime is committed when someone, through a good coming from faith, uses well the evil of lust. Nor can it be said here, as you think: "Let us do evil that good may come from it;"[49] because there is no evil in marriage as marriage. In those who were begotten by parents, the evil which marriage did not produce in them, but only discovered there, does not belong to marriage itself. In the case of the first couple, who had no parents, the discordant evil of carnal concupiscence which marriage uses well was the result of sin, and not of marriage, which does not deserve condemnation from that evil. Why do you ask whether I should call the pleasure of intercourse of Christian spouses modesty or immodesty? Hear my answer: Not the pleasure, but the good use of that evil, is called modesty, and, because of the good use, the evil itself cannot be called immodesty. Immodesty is the shameful use of that same

49. Rom 3.8.

evil, just as virginal modesty is the refraining from using it; therefore, without detriment to conjugal modesty, evil is contracted from evil in birth, and it is to be purged in rebirth.

BOOK FIVE, CHAPTER 9

(39) You do well to distinguish between the lesser good of marriage and the greater good of celibacy, but you are unwilling to put aside this dogma wholly inimical to grace. You say: "Our Lord honored the glory of celibacy with free choice, saying: 'Let him accept it who can'"—as though it were accepted, not by the gift of God, but by freedom of choice. You are silent about what He said earlier: "Not all accept this teaching, but those to whom it has been given."[50] Note what you say and what you leave unsaid. I think your conscience must disturb you, but, if this gives rise to perverted shame, the need to defend a hasty judgment overcomes wholesome fear. You censure only excess and never cease to praise lust itself; nor do you heed or sense or understand that what temperance must oppose, lest it exceed the limits of necessity, is evil.

BOOK FIVE, CHAPTER 10

(43) You boastfully and vainly say I put parents on a par with those who murder their own children, declaring that they cause their offspring to be born under condemnation. While you are elevating yourself on the exultation of your own eloquence, in the furor you create for yourself, you forget God. Why not make these complaints to the very Creator of men, instead of those who beget them, since He is certainly the Author and Creator of all goods; yet He does not cease to create those He has foreknown will burn in eternal fires, nor is aught but goodness imputed to Him because He creates them. Certain infants, even those baptized, He does not take from this life as adopted into the eternal kingdom, and does not confer on them the great benefit given him of whom we read: "He was taken away lest wickedness alter his understanding."[51] Yet, nothing is attributed to God except justice and goodness, by which from goods and evils He makes all things well and rightly. You see how much more understandable it is that noth-

50. Mt 19.12 and 11.   51. Wis 4.11.

ing be imputed to parents, undeniably ignorant of their children's future, except that they choose to have children.

BOOK FIVE, CHAPTER 12

(46) You have many objections to make about my declaration about "Joseph, whose wife was Mary," as I stated according to the Gospel.[52] You try to show that "because there was no intercourse, there was no marriage." By your reasoning, then, when the married cease to have intercourse they are no longer spouses and the cessation will be divorce. Lest this come to pass, the decrepit must according to their power behave as the young, not sparing bodies worn with age from the act in which you, who profess celibacy, take such great joy. In order to remain spouses, let them not think of age, where the incentives of lust are concerned. If this pleases you, look to it. Nevertheless, because human soundness agrees that the motive in taking a wife is the procreation of offspring, regardless of how weakness yields to lust, I note, in addition to the faithfulness which the married owe to each other so that there be no adultery, and the offspring, for whose generation the two sexes are to be united, that a third good, which seems to me to be a sacrament, should exist in the married, above all in those who belong to the people of God, so that there be no divorce from a wife who cannot bear, and that a man not wishing to beget more children give not his wife to another for begetting, as Cato is said to have done.[53] This is why I said the full number of the three goods of marriage is found in what I declared by the Gospel was a marriage: "Faithfulness, because no adultery; offspring, our Lord Christ; and sacrament, because no divorce." And thus my statement that the full number of the goods of marriage, that is, this threefold good, was fulfilled in the parents of Christ does not, as you think, imply I meant to say that whatever is otherwise is evil. I say that there is another way in which marriage is good when offspring can be procreated only through intercourse. If there were another way to procreate, yet the spouses had intercourse, then they evidently must have yielded to lust, and made evil use of evil. But, since the two sexes were

52. DN 1.10.
53. Plutarch, *In vita Catonis;* Lucan 2.

purposely instituted, man can be born only from their union, and thus spouses by their union for this purpose make good use of that evil; if, however, they seek pleasure from lust, this use is excusably evil.

(47) You say: "It was only the common opinion that Joseph was her husband." You would have us think Scripture was merely giving an opinion, not a fact, when it said that the Virgin Mary was his wife. Now, we hold that one of the Evangelists could have written in this way when relating either his own words or those of another man, and thus speaking according to men's opinions; but was the angel, speaking as one person to one person, merely giving an opinion instead of a fact, contrary to his own knowledge and that of his hearer, when he said to Joseph: "Do not be afraid to take to you Mary your wife"? And what was the purpose of listing the generations up to Joseph,[54] if not because the male sex has the place of honor in marriage? You were afraid to meet this argument in the book you are answering.[55] The Evangelist Luke says of our Lord: "Being, as was supposed, the son of Joseph"[56]; because it was so supposed in order that it might be thought He was really begotten through the marriage union of Joseph. Luke wished to remove this false opinion, not to deny, contrary to the angel's testimony, that Mary was Joseph's wife.

(48) You yourself admit that "He received the name husband from the faith of the betrothal." This faith certainly remained inviolate. When he saw the holy Virgin already fruitful with the divine gift, he did not seek another wife, although he would never have sought the Virgin herself if she had not needed a husband. He did not think the bond of conjugal faith should be dissolved because the hope of carnal intercourse had been taken away. But think what you will about that marriage; we do not say, as you calumniate us: "The first spouses were so instituted that they would have been spouses without the carnal union of the two sexes." The point at issue between us is this: whether before sin the flesh lusted against the spirit in Paradise; or whether this does not now take place in spouses, when conjugal modesty itself must restrain the excess of this same

54. Cf. Mt 1.20 and 16.   55. DN 1.12.
56. Lk 3.23.

concupiscence; whether this opposing force to which man may not consent, lest it proceed to its excesses, is not an evil; whether he in whom you deny any evil exists is not born of and with this concupiscence; and whether any man can be delivered from this inborn evil except by regeneration. In these matters your ungodly innovation is silenced by the ancient tradition of the Catholic truth.

BOOK FIVE, CHAPTER 15

(54) When we consider the passing of original sin to all men, we see that because it passes by means of the concupiscence of the flesh, it could not have passed to flesh that a virgin conceived, not through concupiscence. You quote from another book I wrote to Marcellinus, of holy memory, and you attribute to me the statement: "All who were to come from this stock Adam infected in himself." Christ did not come into His mother's womb thence, whence Adam infected all. I shall repeat the most important parts of my argument, since you did not wish to quote them, for reasons that will soon become clear. I said: "By this hidden corruption, that is, his carnal concupiscence, he infected in himself all who were to come from his stock."[57] Thus, he did not infect flesh in whose conception this corruption was not present. The flesh of Christ received mortality from the mortality of His mother's body, because it found her body mortal; it did not contract the taint of original sin, because it did not find the concupiscence of one carnally seminating. But, if He had received only the substance of the flesh from His mother, and not mortality, His flesh not only could not have been sinful flesh; it could not have been the likeness of sinful flesh.

BOOK FIVE, CHAPTER 16

(62) You say: "Marriage is nothing else but the union of bodies." Next you say something true, that "Propagation cannot take place without mutual desire and the union of bodies and the natural act." But, do you deny that adulterers come together with mutual desire in the natural act and the union of bodies? Therefore, you have not given the definition of mar-

57. DPMR 1.10.

riage. Marriage itself is not the same as that without which not even marriage can propagate offspring. Men can be born without marriage, and there can be spouses without the union of bodies; otherwise, to say no more, they will not be spouses when old, and either unable to have intercourse or since they have no hope of offspring, blush and do not wish to perform that act. You see, then, how ill considered is your definition that marriage is nothing else but the union of bodies. It would be more tolerable if you said marriage is not begun except through the union of bodies, because men take wives for the purpose of procreating children, and this cannot be done in any other way. But the union of bodies for the purpose of procreation would have taken place differently if there had been no sin; God forbid we think that that most honest happiness in Paradise always obeyed an aroused lust, and that that peace of soul and body held a cause of internal warfare in the first nature of man. If there was no need either to serve lust or to war against it, then either lust did not exist there or was not such as it is now, for at the present time whoever does not wish to serve lust must war against it; whoever neglects the fight must serve it. Of the two, the one, though praiseworthy, is an affliction; the other is base and wretched. In this world, then, one of these is necessary for the chaste, but in Paradise both were unknown to the blessed.

BOOK SIX, CHAPTER 9

(24) You ask: "Explain how sin can justly be ascribed to that person who did not will to sin and was not able to sin." The commission of personal sins is not the same as the contagion of another's sin, considering a man actually living his own life. If you were not intent on distorting the correct meaning to your perverted notion, you would understand how the Apostle explains this briefly when he says there was one man in whom all sinned. In that one all died, so that another one man might die for all. "Since one died for all, therefore all died"[58] for whom Christ died. Deny, then, that Christ also died for infants, so that you may exclude them from the number of the dead, that is, from the contagion of sins. You ask: "How could a matter

58. 2 Cor 5.15.

of will be mixed with the creation of the seeds?" If this could not happen, we could have no reason to say that infants not yet departed from the body are dead. If Christ also died for them, they also died; "Since one died for all, therefore all died." . . .

BOOK SIX, CHAPTER 14

(43) You would have it seem incredible that "In the womb of a baptized woman, whose body is the temple of God, there be formed a man who must be under the power of the Devil unless he be reborn from God to God," as though it were not more remarkable that God should operate even where He does not dwell. He does not dwell in a body subject to sins, yet He forms a man in the womb of a harlot. He reaches everywhere because of His purity and nothing defiled comes into Him.[59] It is much more remarkable that He sometimes adopts for a son one whom He forms in the womb of an impure woman; and sometimes does not accept for a son him whom He forms in the womb of his own daughter. The one is baptized, by what providence I know not; the other dies suddenly and is not baptized. God, in whose power are all things, receives one whom He has formed in the dwelling of the Devil into fellowship with Christ, and He does not wish that one He formed in His own temple should be in His kingdom. Or, if He wishes it, why does He not do what He wishes? What you are accustomed to say about adults does not apply here, that is, that God wishes and the infant does not wish. Here, where there is no immovable fate, no careless chance, no personal dignity, what remains except the depths of mercy and of truth? From consideration of these two men, the one through whom sin entered into the world, and the other who takes away the sin of the world, let us try, in an incomprehensible matter, to comprehend that all children of this concupiscence of the flesh, no matter whence they are born, deservedly come under the heavy yoke of the children of Adam, and all the children of spiritual grace, no matter whence they are born, without their own merit arrive at the sweet yoke of the children of God. Hence, he has his own condition, whoever is so formed in the body of another, which is the temple of God, that he himself is not the temple of God

59. Cf. Wis 1.4 and 7.24–25.

simply because formed in the temple of God. That the body of his mother is the temple of God is the gift of grace, not of nature, and this grace is not conferred by conception but by regeneration. For, if what is conceived in the mother belonged to her body in such a way as to be regarded part of it, an infant still in the womb would not again be baptized after birth if the mother had been baptized in urgent danger of death. But, as it is, when the infant also is baptized, he is not held to have been baptized twice. He did not belong to his mother's body when he was in her womb; one not the temple of God was created in the temple of God. Thus, an unbeliever is created in a believing woman, and the parents transmitted to him the unbelief which they did not have when he was born from them, but which they themselves had when they were likewise born. They transmitted something no longer in them because of the spiritual seed by which they were regenerated, but it was in the carnal seed by which they generated him.

One of the newly-discovered letters of Augustine gives a brief summary of his mature anti-Pelagian views on the topics of Original Sin and lust. Here, in Epistle 6*, *dated to around 421, he writes to bishop Atticus of Constantinople. The letter shows that, under fire from his Pelagian critics, Augustine had developed a more nuanced position on these issues: he distinguishes between a lawful concupiscence in marriage and "the concupiscence of the flesh," and he concedes that there* might *have been a sinless sexual desire in Eden if the "Fall" had not occurred.*[60]

Augustine sends greetings in the Lord to the most blessed brother, worthy to be received with due reverence, and fellow bishop, Atticus. . . .[61]

---

60. FOTC 81.53–59, *passim.*

61. When John Chrysostom was exiled from Constantinople in June, 404, his immediate successor was Arsacius, the brother of John's predecessor, Nectarius. Arsacius, already an old man, survived for little more than a year and a half. Atticus succeeded him in 406 and served until late 425, gradually repairing the damage done by the cruel treatment shown to John and the angry reaction of John's supporters in Constantinople and in the West.

(3) But that they[62] also slander Catholics is no surprise—if they by this means strive to counter the things [that] are said to prove wrong their poisonous teachings. For what Catholic so defends the right faith against them that he condemns marriage, which the Maker and Creator of the world blessed? What Catholic would call the carnal desire present in marriage the work of the devil, since by means of it the human race would have been propagated even if no one had sinned, in order that the blessing be fulfilled: "Increase and multiply"?[63] By the sin of that man in whom all have sinned, this blessing has not lost the effect of its goodness in that clear, marvelous and praiseworthy fecundity of nature which is there for all to see. What Catholic does not proclaim the works of God in every creature of all soul and flesh and in contemplating them does not burst forth in a hymn to the Creator who was active, not only before the sin, but even now does all good things well?

(4) But they with perverse reasoning confuse with persistent blindness those evils which by reason of sin befall nature with those things that are naturally good, thus praising the Creator of human beings in such a way that they deny that little children need a savior, as if they have nothing evil—this is their most damnable teaching; and they think they can strengthen this vile error by the praise of marriage, saying that marriage is condemned, if what is born of marriage is condemned, unless it is reborn. For they do not see that the good of marriage is one thing, from which good marriage has not fallen away even after sin; but original sin is something else which marriage has not caused and does not cause now, but finds already a fact and uses it well when it does not do with it whatever it likes, but only what is permitted. But these people refuse to consider this, since they have been obsessed with this error, which they prefer to defend rather than to avoid.

(5) Because of this error they do not distinguish the concupiscence associated with marriage, i.e. the concupiscence of conjugal purity, concupiscence for the legitimate engendering of children, or the concupiscence of the social bond by which each sex is tied to the other, from concupiscence of the flesh

62. The Pelagians.   63. Gn 1.28.

which hankers after the illicit as well as the licit indifferently and through the concupiscence of marriage which uses it well is restrained from the illicit and permitted only the licit. All chastity fights against this force which wars against the law of the mind,[64] both of spouses that they may make good use of it, and of the continent and of holy virgins that they in a better and more glorious way may not make use of it at all. Not distinguishing this concupiscence of the flesh, therefore, in which the sole desire is for sexual relations, from the concupiscence of marriage in which there is the duty of engendering, they most brazenly praise the former, concerning which the first human beings were ashamed, when they covered with fig leaves those organs which before the sin had not been objects of shame;[65] for they were naked and unashamed so that we may understand that this movement by which they were put to shame was conceived in human nature at the same time as death. For then they had a reason for shame, when they also began to have the necessity of dying. They proclaim with such great praises that this concupiscence of the flesh must be prudently and soberly distinguished from the concupiscence involved in marriage so that they think that, even if no one had sinned in paradise, without it they were not able to procreate children in the body of this life just as now they are not procreated without it in the body of this death, from which the Apostle longs to be freed through Jesus Christ.

(6) Whence it happens that so great an absurdity follows this opinion of theirs, coming, as it does, from such unreflective ignorance that no matter with how great effrontery the human face may be hardened, even they are not able to uphold it without qualification. For if that concupiscence of the flesh existed in paradise before the sin, which we know has so disordered a movement that by the restraints of chastity it must be kept back from all usage, or turned by the good of marriage to a good usage, although it is in itself evil, undoubtedly even in that place of such great blessedness there would be two alternatives: either it would be submitted to shamefully, if as many times as there was the motion, so often would he have intercourse with

64. Cf. Rom 7.23. 65. Cf. Gn 3.7.

his wife with no need of begetting children, but in order that the appetite for pleasure be gratified, even if his wife were already pregnant; or it must be fought against by the strength of abstinence lest he be dragged down to such filthy things. Let them choose which of these two pleases them. For if the lust of the flesh was submitted to, rather than made to submit, then there was no moral freedom there; if, however, it was forced to submit lest he be found to submit to it, then there was no calm and peaceful bliss. No matter which one of these is chosen, the happy beauty or the beautiful happiness of paradise is abandoned.

(7) Who does not see this? Who would contradict this most obvious truth except by a most brazen obstinacy? It remains therefore that either this concupiscence of the flesh, which we feel disturbing us with such unruly and inordinate desires against our will even when there is no need, did not exist there, although there was the concupiscence of marriage maintaining the peaceful love of spouses and just as the will commands the hands and feet to move to do appropriate things, so it would have commanded the genital organs to acts of generation that in paradise children might have been sown in a marvelous way without the trials of the lust of the flesh, just as they would have been born in a marvelous way without the pangs of birth; or, if that concupiscence of the flesh did exist there, it was not such as now that they who fight against it with chastity either of the married, the widow, or the virgin, believe it to be, viz., most burdensome and hateful. For it forces itself in where it is not needed and, by insistent or even wicked desires, it seduces the hearts of even the faithful and the saints; it forces itself in by these turbulent movements even if we do not consent in the slightest but, on the contrary, fight back; still by an altogether more holy desire, if it were possible, we would not want to have these things in us, as one day indeed they will not. For this is the perfection of the good, which the apostle indicated was lacking in the saints in this life thus far, when he said: "I can will what is right, but I cannot complete it."[66] For he does not say simply "do," but "complete," since a man does what is good

66. Rom 7.18.

by not giving in to such desires, but he does not complete it because he still has them nonetheless. He says: "For I do not do the good I want, but the evil I do not want is what I do."[67] For indeed he was not doing evil by presenting his members for fulfilling evil desires, but he said this of the lustful movements themselves, to which even if he did not consent nor do what they urged, still, he was doing what he was unwilling to have just by having them. Finally, he adds: "Now if I do what I do not want . . ."[68] i.e., although I do not consent to the concupiscence—I do not want to lust but I do it anyway—"it is no longer I that do it, but the sin which dwells in me."[69] The guilt of this sin is brought on by generation, is taken away by regeneration by which there is the forgiveness of all sins. Still some of its power and a certain feeling of deadly contagion remain in the corruptible and mortal body even when the guilt has been taken away, against which the person who has been reborn fights, if he is to make progress. For even if he embrace, not total continence, but conjugal chastity, he will also fight against this concupiscence of the flesh, lest he commit adultery, lest he fornicate and be corrupted by any death-dealing and wicked vices: lastly he will not use even his wife intemperately when, with her consent, he will have to abstain from sexual intercourse for a time to have time for prayer and then they will go back to it again, "lest Satan tempt them through lack of self-control,"[70] which the apostle says to them is "by way of concession, not of command."[71] Certain ones, giving little consideration to this, thought that marriage itself had been allowed "by way of concession." But it is not so; otherwise, God forbid, matrimony would be a sin. For when a concession is made, it is recognized at once that a fault is forgiven; but it is sexual intercourse, not that to which a concern for begetting children leads, but that to which the inability to contain the drive to satisfy lust constrains which the apostle allows to spouses between themselves "by way of concession" lest damnable sins be committed, so long as the concession is not stretched too far. Even if some spouses are standing out by vir-

tue of such great conjugal purity that they have sexual relations
for the sole purpose of begetting children and now, baptized
and reborn, they live accordingly, nevertheless, any child born
to them through that concupiscence of the flesh which though
not good in itself they make good use of through the good
concupiscence of marriage, still contracts original sin. And
what is not removed except by rebirth alone, accompanies without a doubt the one born unless he is also reborn, just as the
foreskin which is removed only by circumcision accompanies
the son of a circumcised man, unless the son too is circumcised.

(8) Therefore this concupiscence of the flesh, if it existed in
paradise so that by means of it children were begotten to fulfill
the blessing of marriage by the multiplication of human beings,
was not the same kind of carnal concupiscence we experience
now, when its movements covet indifferently what is licit and
illicit. It would be carried away into many vile things if it were
permitted to go wherever it is moved. Against this type of concupiscence we must struggle, if chastity is to be preserved. But
if concupiscence had existed in paradise, it would have had to
be of a different type, in which the flesh would never have
lusted against the spirit,[72] but would not go beyond the inclination of the will in a wonderful harmony; it would never even
be present unless there were a need, it would never force itself
into a person's conscious thoughts with its inordinate and illicit
attractions; it would have had nothing disgraceful which would
have to be restrained by the reins of temperance or fought
against by the efforts of virtue; on those occasions when it was
necessary, it would have followed the person's will with ready
and compliant obedience. But since this is definitely *not* the way
concupiscence is now and it is necessary for chastity to overcome its adversary, let them admit that it has been corrupted
by the sin, so that by its movements, they who previously were
naked and unashamed are now put to shame. Let them not
marvel that only the son of a virgin, whom they cannot say was
conceived by the concupiscence of the flesh, did not contract
original sin. Forgive me because of the length of this letter. I
have burdened your holy thoughts, not that I might make you

72. Cf. Gal 5.17.

more learned, but that I might refute the calumnies they are spreading in your region.

Thus Augustine's developed sexual ethic, which was crucial for all later Catholic thinking on marriage and reproduction, was stimulated by his responses to the opponents he confronted: Manicheans, extreme ascetics as well as anti-ascetics, and Pelagians. He sought to develop a sexual and marital ethic that praised the goodness of creation and of reproduction, while upholding the sinfulness of sexual lust. Moreover, marriage involved more than procreation and the containment of lust, for Augustine: it involved a partnership of faithful spouses in a "sacramental bond" that neither adultery nor separation could break. In his time, he sought to combat heretical opinions—whether of the Manicheans or of the Pelagians—while maintaining a moderate stance on sexual and marital issues within the atmosphere of raging debates over asceticism in his era. Especially in his later years, he was concerned to insist on the radical nature of human sinfulness, even while he praised the goodness of human creation and God's justice in his dealings with it. Among our contemporaries, some may laud Augustine's efforts and others may decry them: all, however, must concede his importance in the development of Christian views on marriage, reproduction, and human sexuality.

GENERAL INDEX

Aaron, 73
Abandonment, 48–49
Abortion, 1
Abraham, 56–58
Abstinence, sexual, 54, 69
Accusations by sinners, 60
Adam and Eve, 3, 5, 38, 44, 72
Adam's guilt, 74
Adeodatus, 4, 17, 18–19
Adultery, 88, 96; as caused by aban-
    donment, 48–49; and conspiracy,
    35; as continence, 35–36; and di-
    vorce, 6; defined, 46; and fidelity,
    47; compared to marriage, 69; as
    mortal sin, 47; for procreation,
    49, 56; against whom it is commit-
    ted, 20; by whom it is committed,
    89; as worse than a broken vow,
    24
Almsgiving, 28, 29
Ambrose, St., 4
Anna, 30, 51, 60, 80–81, 83
Apocrypha, 2
Apparel, decency of, 29–30
Asceticism, 2, 3, 8; of Augustine,
    41
Atticus, Bishop of Constantinople,
    99
Auditors, Manichean, 5, 32
Augustine: and Ambrose, 4; accusa-
    tion of over-ascetic sexual ethic
    against, 41; and Adeodatus, 4,
    18–19; adolescence of, 13; be-
    trothal of, 17–18; first concubine
    of, 4–5, 17–19; second concubine
    of, 18–19; conversion of, 19; edu-
    cation of, 15; early life of, 4; as
    Manichean Auditor, 5, 32; oppo-

nents of 8–10. See also Mani-
    cheans and Pelagians

Baptism: as acceptance into heaven,
    98; of Augustine, 17; as needed
    by children, 100, 104; as not only
    key to heaven, 93; forgiveness in,
    70; graces as not passed to de-
    scendants, 87; creating "new peo-
    ple," 71; sexual shame after, 75–
    76; sin committed after, 7, 9
Belief, 55
Blood relationship, 43
Body: as evil, 3, 33; as mortal yet
    undying, 44–45; as temple of God,
    98–99; as opposed to soul, 34

Celibacy, 3, 14, 42; in the Apocry-
    phal Acts, 2; as a choice, 93; Je-
    rome's teachings on, 42; in mar-
    riage, 51–52, 94; Paul's teachings
    on, 2, 8; reasons for, 52
Chastity, 20, 39, 57, 82; crown of
    marriage, 54; fight of, against
    lust, 97, 101, 104; as gift from
    God, 79, 83; humility in, 60; in
    marriage, 89; second and third
    century praise of, 2; of virgins,
    66; of widows, 65–66
Children, 17, 39; custody of, after
    divorce, 31; as inheritors of sin, 9,
    87, 91, 96, 98; as first good of
    marriage, 1, 45; as needing bap-
    tism, 100, 104; possibilities of,
    prior to Original Sin, 44, 78; as
    reason for sexual intercourse, 19–
    20, 36, 43; as solution for death,
    44

INDEX OF HOLY SCRIPTURE

St. Augustine on Marriage and Sexuality was composed in
Baskerville by Brevis Press, Bethany, Connecticut; printed on 6o–pound
Writers Natural by McNaughton & Gunn Lithographers, Saline, Michigan;
bound by John Dekker & Sons, Grand Rapids, Michigan; and designed and
produced by Kachergis Book Design, Pittsboro, North Carolina.